CAMPAIGN 350

NIERSTEIN AND OPPENHEIM 1945

Patton Bounces the Rhine

RUSS RODGERS

ILLUSTRATED BY DARREN TAN
Series editor Marcus Cowper

OSPREY PUBLISHING
Bloomsbury Publishing Plc
PO Box 883, Oxford, OX1 9PL, UK
1385 Broadway, 5th Floor, New York, NY 10018, USA
E-mail: info@ospreypublishing.com
www.ospreypublishing.com

OSPREY is a trademark of Osprey Publishing Ltd

First published in Great Britain in 2020

A catalog record for this book is available from the British Library.

ISBN: PB 9781472840400; eBook 9781472840417; ePDF 9781472840387; XML 9781472840394

20 21 22 23 24   10 9 8 7 6 5 4 3 2 1

Maps by www.bounford.com
3D BEVs by Paul Kime
Index by Sandra Shotter
Typeset by PDQ Digital Media Solutions, Bungay, UK
Printed and bound in India by Replika Press Private Ltd.

MIX
Paper from responsible sources
FSC® C016779
www.fsc.org

Artist's note

Readers can find out more about the work of battlescene illustrator Darren Tan at the following website:

https://www.artstation.com/wraithdt

Osprey Publishing supports the Woodland Trust, the UK's leading woodland conservation charity.

To find out more about our authors and books visit **www.ospreypublishing.com**. Here you will find extracts, author interviews, details of forthcoming events, and the option to sign up for our newsletter.

Author's acknowledgments

I would like to thank Darren Neely for running down photos for me from National Archives; Charles Lemons for years of support while at the Patton Museum and beyond, in providing unique photos and other materials; Tom Buffenbarger of the Military History Institute, for providing so much material for use on staff rides both past and future; Ericka Loze-Hudson and the team at the Infantry School's Donovan Library, for help in running down After Action Reports and official histories; and my colleagues and friends Chuck White and Jeff Miller, Army Command historians, who have always encouraged me to press forward with research.

Abbreviations

MP	Military Police
OB	Oberbefehlshaber (Army Command)
OKW	Oberkommando der Wehrmacht (High Command of the Armed Forces)
ROTC	Reserve Officers Training Corps
SCAF	Supreme Command Allied Forces
SHAEF	Supreme Headquarters Allied Expeditionary Force
TAC	Tactical Air Command

Dedication

This volume is dedicated to my wife Alina and daughter Haylee, who endure so much while I'm away or writing.

Key to military symbols

Army Group · Army · Corps · Division · Brigade · Regiment · Battalion
Company/Battery · Platoon · Section · Squad · Infantry · Artillery · Cavalry
Airborne · Unit HQ · Air defense · Air Force · Air mobile · Air transportable · Amphibious
Antitank · Armor · Air aviation · Bridging · Engineer · Headquarters · Maintenance
Medical · Missile · Mountain · Navy · Nuclear, biological, chemical · Ordnance · Parachute
Reconnaissance · Signal · Supply · Transport movement · Rocket artillery · Air defense artillery

Key to unit identification

Unit identifier · Parent unit · Commander · (+) with added elements · (-) less elements

PREVIOUS PAGE
The bridge over the Rhine at Nierstein, built by Third US Army engineers. (NARA)

CONTENTS

ORIGINS OF THE CAMPAIGN

The Allied campaign across France, while moving faster than originally planned once their forces had broken out of the invasion lodgment in Normandy, caused a logistical nightmare that served to retard further advances into Germany. Even as the Allies strove to strengthen their logistical situation by rebuilding the French railroads and at last opening the Belgian port of Antwerp, the Germans threw a monkey wrench into Allied plans with their December offensive in the Ardennes, followed by their January 1945 offensive in Alsace. Yet, even though German efforts temporarily stymied the Allied drive through the Westwall, commonly referred to as the Siegfried Line, these offensive operations cost the Wehrmacht dearly in both men and materiel.

The production of tanks for the Germans bear this out. Despite the Allied bombing campaign, Reich Minister of Armaments and War Production Albert Speer was able to bring tank production to its maximum level by late 1944. However, the failed offensives in the West squandered much of this production, as the Wehrmacht was unable to recover most of its battle-damaged equipment when it fell back to its start points. Thus, the increased production at best only partly replaced what was lost. Moreover, a misguided German effort to thwart Allied air supremacy in the West, known as Operation *Bodenplatte* (*Baseplate*), resulted in not only the loss of over 300 German aircraft but also many irreplaceable pilots.

Making these problems worse were the ongoing Soviet offensives in the East. In December, Soviet forces pressed into Hungary, threatening Budapest and one of the last remaining oil reserves available to Germany near Nagykanisza, southwest of Lake Balaton. German counterattacks to stop these advances met both fierce Soviet resistance and horrendous weather that turned roads and fields into morasses, and despite these efforts Budapest was surrounded on December 24. With the assault in the Ardennes still ongoing, the Oberkommando der Wehrmacht (OKW—High Command of the Armed Forces) had to strip other fronts in the East to find a reserve to attempt to relieve the city and secure the oil fields. Operation *Konrad* was developed to relieve the city, and more ambitious operations were planned for the near future. *Konrad* was launched from the northwest of the city from January 1 to 8, 1945, and managed to advance two-thirds of the 45km to the edge of the German lines before stalling. *Konrad II* and *III*, were launched more from the south later in January, and again closed in on the city, only to grind to a halt through a combination of weather difficulties and growing Soviet resistance. To make matters worse, the Soviets launched their own offensive

Field Marshal Montgomery (right, foreground) discusses operational execution with Brigadier-General William H. Simpson (left) on March 25, 1945, after the initiation of Operation *Plunder*. Lieutenant-General Bradley, 12th US Army Group commander (center, rear) looks on, along with Major-General John Anderson of the US XVI Corps (left, rear) and British Field Marshal Alanbrooke (right, rear). Montgomery demanded up to 12 additional American divisions for his operations, but relented when Eisenhower insisted that Bradley command the American forces side by side with Montgomery. (NARA)

into Poland on January 12, and the front collapsed, as Generaloberst Heinz Guderian had predicted, like a house of cards.

Hitler's stance up to this time was that the Eastern Front was going to have to fend for itself. But this series of disasters convinced him that the Ardennes Offensive needed to be abandoned and significant forces shifted to the East. Watching the crisis build, on January 16 the OKW sent orders to Generalfeldmarschall Gerd von Rundstedt to pull most of 6.Panzer-Armee from the line and have them refitted for future action. By the end of the month, these forces were rail loaded and on the move to Hungary, and thus Rundstedt lost a significant body of combat troops for his exhausted front. With the loss of 6.Panzer-Armee, 5.Panzer-Armee shifted northward, along with its armor and mechanized troops. The suspension of Operation *Nordwind*, an assault along the Franco-German border between Sarreguemines and Wissembourg, completed the depletion of armor in the West. All told, five SS-Panzer divisions, with two elite brigades (1., 2., 9., 10., and 12.Panzer divisions, and Führer-Begleit-Brigade and Grenadier-Brigade), along with 21.Panzer-Division and the newly reformed 25.Panzergrenadier-Division were sent east, constituting over 50 percent of the mechanized strength to Rundstedt's command. Besides the Panzer units, he also lost infantry divisions, all told losing 16 divisions and their equivalents, with many being the best equipped on hand. This constituted an almost one-third reduction of the entire force in the West. And with the need to protect the Ruhr industrial district, what was left of Rundstedt's armor was mostly concentrated to the north of Koblenz. Only 2.Panzer-Division, still licking its wounds after its mauling in the Ardennes by its opposite number in the US Army, and 17.SS-Panzergrenadier-Division "Götz von Berlichingen"

A sign of the coming end was the increasing prevalence of white flags and sheets flown in German towns, such as here in Polch, as civilians attempted to avoid having what little was left being destroyed in combat. In some instances, German civilians aided both German and Allied troops in identifying and removing explosives and roadblocks so as to keep the war as far away as possible. Nevertheless, some diehard German commanders strove to suppress such displays of collaboration, and pressed civilians into building fortifications or service in the Volksturm. (NARA)

remained south of Koblenz—two weary mechanized divisions to act as a fire brigade for two-thirds of the Western Front.

In February 1945, the entire Western Front seemed to explode. Coordinated advances by the Allied armies along the whole front hammered their way through the crumbling edifice of what was left of Heeresgruppe West. Operation *Grenade* saw Montgomery's 21st Army Group, supported by the Ninth US Army, cut its way to the Rhine River by March 11. Patton's Third US Army pushed across the Schnee Eifel and the western Palatinate to reach the Moselle River by early March. But the thrust that gained the headlines was that of Hodges' First US Army with Operation *Lumberjack*, whose 9th Armored Division captured the Ludendorff Bridge at Remagen, on March 7. Along with the French Second Army and Patch's Seventh US Army, who were positioned along the upper Rhine River, these advances left a large German salient protruding from along the Moselle River to Trier, and then along the Franco-German border.

In the East, German offensives in Hungary had marginal gains but were stopped by appalling weather and stiffening Soviet resistance. Moreover, Soviet forces pushed through Poland, cut off East Prussia from the rest of the Reich, and threw bridgeheads across the Oder River. They were now close to 80km from Berlin. In addition, the fall of much of the Saar region and Silesia had dealt a crippling blow to the German industrial effort, and any hope of producing sufficient materiel to continue prosecuting the war had been dashed.

The various German offensives cost the Wehrmacht heavily in men and materiel. The last truly potent reserve had been expended in Hungary and the Western Front had been denuded of any mechanized reserve whatsoever. For Germany and the Wehrmacht, the final catastrophe was about to begin.

CHRONOLOGY

1944

November 3	Third US Army develops offensive plans to cross the Rhine River between Oppenheim and Mannheim.
November 28	The Scheldt Estuary is at last cleared by British forces, and the first ships arrive at the port of Antwerp. Allied logistics are now assured for a drive into Germany.
December 16	The Germans launch their last major offensive, codenamed *Wacht am Rhein* (*Watch on the Rhine*), in the West through the Ardennes Forest.
December 26	Elements of Patton's Third US Army break the siege of Bastogne.
December 31	German forces launch Operation *Nordwind*, an offensive to clear US forces from portions of northern Alsace.

1945

January 1	The German Luftwaffe attempts a massive ground attack strike against Allied airfields with Operation *Bodenplatte*. Despite marginal success, the cost in aircraft and pilots is crippling for the Luftwaffe.
January 7	Hitler calls off the Ardennes Offensive. The lion's share of German armor reserves are sent to the Eastern Front.
January 12	On the Eastern Front, the Soviets begin their Vistula–Oder Offensive. German forces are swept from Poland.
January 25	The *Nordwind* offensive is at last fully contained. German forces are on the defensive.
February 13	On the Eastern Front, German and Hungarian resistance in Budapest ends with the last breakout attempt crushed. The siege of Budapest had prompted a number of major German offensives to secure its relief.
February 22	Operation *Grenade* begins, with the British 21st Army Group, supported by the Ninth US Army, driving for the Rhine River.
March 1	Operation *Lumberjack* begins, as the First US Army begins its drive to the Rhine.
March 2	Elements of the US XX Corps capture Trier.
March 6	On the Eastern Front, the Germans launch the Lake Balaton Offensive, called *Frühlingserwachen (Spring Awakening)*. The last operational reserves of the Wehrmacht are expended.

March 7	Elements of the 9th Armored Division under the First US Army capture the Ludendorff Bridge on the Rhine at Remagen. The bridgehead is slowly expanded and the area begins to draw in virtually every German reserve unit on the Western Front.
March 13–14	Patton's XII Corps begins its offensive across the Moselle River, the northern offensive to trap German forces in the Saar-Palatinate Triangle.
March 15	The Seventh US Army begins Operation *Undertone*, comprising a drive to the north and east to trap German forces in the Saar-Palatinate Triangle.
March 22–23	Elements of the US 5th Infantry Division begin a surprise crossing of the Rhine at Nierstein–Oppenheim. German resistance steadily crumbles.
March 24	Montgomery's 21st Army Group, with Operation *Plunder*, crosses the Rhine near Wesel.
April 1	Elements of the Ninth and First US armies seal off the Ruhr Pocket (also called the Rose Pocket, named for the commander of the 3rd Armored Division recently killed in action).
April 16	On the Eastern Front, Soviet forces launch their final major offensive to cross the Oder River and capture Berlin.
April 18	The Ruhr Pocket surrenders.
April 19	Elements of Patton's Third US Army reach the border of Czechoslovakia.
April 30	Hitler commits suicide in the bunker of the Reich Chancellery.
May 8	Victory in Europe Day; German forces surrender, though sporadic fighting in isolated areas will continue for almost a month.

OPPOSING COMMANDERS

GERMAN

SS-Oberst-Gruppenführer Paul Hausser (1880–1972) took command of Heeresgruppe G, which covered the southern half of the Western Front, in January 1945. Hausser began his military career with the German Army in World War I, and was part of the interwar Reichswehr until his retirement in 1932 as a Generalleutnant (a two-star equivalent in the US Army). He came out of retirement to help create the Waffen-SS, and led the SS-Verfügungs-Division during the invasion of France in 1940. Later reflagged as 2.SS-Panzer-Division "Das Reich," Hausser led this division into the Soviet Union until he was severely wounded in October 1941, losing his right eye. After recovery, he led the newly created SS-Panzer-Korps during the Third Battle of Kharkov and the Battle of Kursk in 1943. Reflagged as II.SS-Panzer-Korps, Hausser and his command were sent to the West immediately after the Normandy invasion. He was tapped to be the new commander of 7.Armee on June 29, 1944. Again severely wounded in August, he did not return to field command until January 1945, first leading Oberkommando Oberrhein and then Heeresgruppe G. It appears that he fell out of favor with Kesselring and was relieved of command on April 4, spending the remainder of the war as part of Kesselring's Heeresgruppe West staff. Known as "Papa" Hausser to his men, he was arguably the most competent senior leader of the Waffen-SS, and was the holder of the Knights Cross with Oak Leaves and Swords.

General Hans Felber (1889–1962) led 7.Armee from February 22, 1945, having previously exercised a rear-area command along the upper Rhine River. Felber served in World War I as a junior officer, and postwar was involved in the Freikorps movement before serving in the Reichswehr. By 1934, he had been promoted to Oberst, and briefly was the commandant of the Kriegsakademie (War Academy). In 1937, he was a Generalmajor (a brigadier-general by American standards), and served as the chief of staff of various commands before receiving command of XIII.Armee-Korps on October 25, 1940. In doing this, he bypassed

SS-Oberst-Gruppenführer Paul Hausser, commander of Heeresgruppe G, was responsible for almost two-thirds of the Western Front, and yet had the bare minimum of tanks and assault guns. He and his army commanders told Kesselring, who was the Oberbefehlshaber West, that an American attack in the Saar-Palatinate would jeopardize both 7.Armee and 1.Armee, as well as the defense of the Rhine. (Bundesarchiv, Bild 101III-Hoffmann-013-17)

General Hans Felber (left) commanded 7.Armee during Patton's drive to the Rhine. Kesselring was greatly disturbed by what he considered to be Felber's lack of energy in properly defending the river, and had him sacked on March 25. After the war, Felber was put on trial for war crimes related to his involvement in the deportation of the Jews in Lodz, but the trial was discontinued and he was released. (Bundesarchiv, Bild 101I-027-1476-38A)

Patton, here as a four-star general at the end of the war, commanded the Third US Army from the time of its activation in Normandy until the war's end. There is a considerable divergence between the real Patton and the caricature created after the war in popular media. He has been cited by German generals as the one Allied commander they truly feared because of his drive and unpredictability. (US Army Signal Corps/The General George Patton Museum)

command at both regimental and divisional levels. He led the XIII. and later LXXXIII.Armee-Korps in Russia until assigned to command a detachment to fight partisans in Serbia. In 1945, Felber held command of 7.Armee until relieved on March 25. As a prisoner of war, Felber was tried for war crimes, but the charges were dropped and he lived out his last years near Frankfurt/ Main. Felber does not stand out as an above-average military leader, and it is interesting that he somehow managed to avoid several layers of command responsibility. Kesselring was not impressed with him, later expressing astonishment that he appeared to be quite torpid in his preparations to oppose Patton's crossing of the Rhine. Nevertheless, it should be noted that it was Kesselring who disregarded Felber's express contention that holding exposed positions in the Saar-Palatinate Triangle would result in the virtual destruction of his 7.Armee prior to Patton's Rhine crossing. He was a holder of the Knights Cross.

US

Lieutenant-General George S. Patton, Jr. (1885–1945) needs little introduction to most students of military history. Yet, he is also the subject of numerous myths and legends that have made the popular view of his life a caricature. Patton graduated from the US Military Academy at West Point in 1909. He served as General John Pershing's aide during the American Expeditionary incursion into Mexico in 1916, and later led the first American tank force in France during World War I, being seriously wounded and receiving the Distinguished Service Cross. Though an ardent lover of horse cavalry, Patton transferred to the new Armor Force. As war clouds grew in Europe, most other officers in Patton's class were retired by Chief of Staff of the Army General George C. Marshall, but Marshall saw in Patton an exception, being both vigorous and driven despite his older age. Patton commanded the Western Task Force during the Allied invasion of Western North Africa in November 1942, and was tapped to rebuild the shaken US II Corps after the setback at Kasserine Pass. He would lead the Seventh US Army in the invasion of Sicily, but several incidents where he slapped enlisted soldiers almost led to his being relieved and prevented him from heading up the invasion of Normandy. He was instead tasked to lead the Third US Army, which he did with distinction to the end of the war, earning four stars by 1945.

While often portrayed in popular media as a braggart and threatening loudmouth, Patton was adroit at keeping confidences, and was particularly careful to protect his subordinates, even after significant failure, from public criticism. He also owned a library of over 400 books on military history, many of them cross-annotated with his own notes, thus making him arguably the most studied senior commander on the Allied side in World War II. He was assessed by the Germans as the most dangerous opponent to face, being innovative, driven, and unpredictable in action, possessing an uncanny understanding of human psychology. Patton was critically injured in a car accident in December 1945, dying shortly after. Today his remains are buried in the Luxembourg cemetery at Hamm with many of his Third US Army soldiers who fell in action, most during the Battle of the Bulge.

Major-General Manton Eddy (left), commander of Patton's US XII Corps, Patton, and Major-General Willard Paul talk tactics during the Lorraine campaign in late 1944. Eddy could at times be over cautious, but under Patton's leadership became a dependable and effective corps commander. Paul, with a decided academic bent, specialized in training and transformed his 26th Infantry Division into one of Patton's best. It was Paul's troops, along with the 4th Armored Division, that made the decisive drive to lift the siege of Bastogne during the Battle of the Bulge. (US Army Signal Corps/The General George Patton Museum)

Major-General Manton S. Eddy (1892–1962), commanded the US XII Corps from the Normandy breakout up to the closing days of the war. Eddy entered the US Army as an enlisted man in 1916, and was commissioned two years later as a second lieutenant. He led a machine-gun company during World War I, being wounded in action. Between the wars, Eddy attended the usual service schools and served on the Infantry Board at Fort Benning, GA. In December 1941, he took command of the 114th Infantry Regiment, which was part of the New Jersey National Guard and assigned to the 44th Infantry Division. By August 1942, Eddy was in command of the 9th Infantry Division, leading it in North Africa, Sicily, and the early part of the Normandy invasion, where he assisted in the capture of Cherbourg. When Major-General Gilbert Cook became ill in August 1944, Eddy took command of XII Corps, leading it until he too had to relinquish command due to illness. After World War II, Eddy was promoted to three-star general and ran the Command and General Staff College, and then led the Seventh US Army in the occupation of Germany. He retired in March 1953. Eddy could demonstrate indecisiveness and nervousness in fluid situations, but still proved himself to be a stable and effective combat leader, especially under the guiding hand of someone like Patton.

Major-General William M. Hoge (1894–1979), commanded the elite 4th Armored Division in the last months of the war. He graduated from West Point in 1916, along with Horace McBride, who would later command the 80th Infantry Division. Commissioned as an engineer, Hoge participated in the St Mihiel and Meuse-Argonne offensives in World War I, the latter as a battalion commander where he earned the Distinguished Service Cross. Between the wars,

he pursued an education in civil engineering, graduating from the Massachusetts Institute of Technology. He commanded an engineer battalion of the Philippine Scouts in 1935, and later served as General Douglas MacArthur's Chief of Engineers. After the attack on Pearl Harbor, Hoge was promoted to one-star general and assigned as the commanding general for the Alaskan–Canadian (Alcan) Highway, completing the essentials of the project in an astonishing nine months in October 1942. By November 1944, Hoge was called upon to lead CCB of the 9th Armored Division, guiding it through the darkest days of the Battle of the Bulge when defending the "goose egg" around St Vith. A few months later, it was Hoge's CCB that executed the drive on Remagen that led to the capture of the Ludendorff Bridge and the first crossing of the Rhine River on March 7, 1945. Two weeks later, he took command of the 4th Armored Division, and was promoted to two-star general on May 2, 1945. He later commanded the IX Corps during the Korean War, and served as the commander of the United States Army

William Hoge had led CCB of the 9th Armored Division when it captured the Remagen Bridge, and prior to this had been tasked with defending the St Vith "goose egg" during the early, dark days of the German offensive in the Ardennes. He took command of the elite 4th Armored Division on March 21, two days before his tanks crossed the Rhine. Hoge is the only senior leader, and possibly the only soldier on either side, to participate in both the Remagen and Oppenheim crossings. (Military History Institute)

Europe (USAREUR). Promoted to four-star rank, Hoge retired in 1955. Hoge was fiercely loyal to his subordinates and was capable of making rapid and well-informed decisions under significant stress, making him a valuable asset to any who served with him.

Major-General S. Leroy Irwin (1893–1955) graduated from West Point in 1915, along with such notables as Dwight D. Eisenhower, Omar Bradley, and James Van Fleet. Being commissioned in the cavalry, Irwin participated in the Punitive Expedition into Mexico in 1916, but saw no overseas service during World War I. Transferring to the artillery, he became a Reserve Officers Training Corps (ROTC) professor at Yale University in the early 1920s, and later did a tour of duty in the Philippines. During the Allied invasion of North Africa, he served as the artillery commander for the 9th Infantry Division. On June 3, 1943, he was promoted to two-star general and took command of the 5th Infantry Division later that month. He led the division almost

to the end of the war before taking command of XII Corps. After the war, he commanded occupation forces in Austria, and retired from the army in 1952 as a three-star general. Irwin was not necessarily a spectacular commander, but instead exhibited solid workmanship in the handling of his division, and was often handed difficult assignments, such as the capture of some of the fortifications of Metz. He and his staff became particularly adept at river crossing operations, making his division the obvious choice for the surprise Rhine River crossing.

OPPOSING FORCES

After the Allied landings on the Normandy coast, the drive across France revealed conflicting aspects of how the Allied armies, especially the Americans, and the Wehrmacht viewed modern warfare. What was to transpire along the Rhine River in early 1945 was in many ways the final culmination of methods, by both the Allies and Germans, that were refined in France and along the Western German frontier. The view taken by many historians is that the Allies ultimately triumphed due to materiel superiority assisted by massive doses of airpower. Like all misconceptions, this viewpoint is based on a certain degree of truth laced with large measures of fiction. There is no doubt that the Allies had materiel superiority, but this is certainly not the complete story.

There were few who doubted that the Wehrmacht displayed an edge in tactical ability and small-unit leadership, an edge that they would maintain almost to the end of the war. But in contrast, the Allied forces, particularly the Americans, demonstrated a level of operational ability unseen since the early days of the conflict. Indeed, the aspect of the operational art is largely misunderstood, and thus this edge possessed by American forces is typically overlooked. While positioned between strategy and tactics, there is no clear delineation between them. Strategy is defined as the overall concept and plan to achieve final victory, while tactics are the methods by which units actually engage enemy forces in the field and defeat them. However, when it comes to the operational level, there is no consensus on what this means or how it is even conducted. For example, Michael Howard has referred to the operational level as the "grey area between strategy and tactics," and that "strategy is about thinking and planning. Operations are about doing."[1] Unfortunately, this definition still does not bring us any resolution. So where lies the operational art, and how was the American army superior in conducting it?

Probably one of the best ways to define the operational level is not by unit size, such as at the division, corps, or army level, but rather by the relative amount of logistical independence a combat force has in the field. The more logistical independence, the greater possible presence of the operational art. This definition, if accepted as reasonable, goes a long way in explaining the gray area between strategy and tactics, for the level of logistical independence will vary considerably at any given time. In addition to logistical independence, units engaged in the operational level must be capable of achieving a significant decision against opposing forces. Therefore, to fight at the operational level, the force in question must have

1   Prologue to John Andreas Olsen and Martin van Creveld (eds.), *The Evolution of Operational Art: From Napoleon to the Present*, Oxford University Press (2011).

OPPOSITE
Major-General Leroy Irwin (pointing) ably led the 5th Infantry Division in the drive across France and into Germany. To the left in dark waist jacket is Major-General Walton Walker, commander of the US XX Corps. Irwin's division became specialists in river crossings, while Walker, who emulated Patton, was known as a speed demon when riding in his command car. Ironically, he would later be killed in a car accident during the Korean War when his car slid on an icy road and collided with a South Korean Army truck. Here, Irwin is explaining how his division will subdue the fortifications of Metz in November 1944. (US Army Signal Corps/The General George Patton Museum)

Contrary to German practice, which emphasized training at the regiment or division level, American forces engaged in large-scale corps and army level exercises for several years before being deployed to Europe. This made the US Army potentially the most effective operational force of the war. In the hands of a dynamic commander like Patton, these qualities would be brought to the forefront. Here, M4 Sherman tanks and their crews prepare for a major exercise in the Mojavi Desert early in the war. (US Army Signal Corps/The General George Patton Museum)

the quality and striking power sufficient to defeat an enemy in the field. These two factors, logistical independence and ability to create a decision, demonstrate that the operational art can be practiced in a wide range of circumstances and at various levels of command.

In the early part of World War II, the German Panzer force was an operational asset largely because they had a tremendous level of logistical independence from higher authority, and because the force when massed could generate a clear decision on the battlefield. When the Panzer and motorized formations of Heeresgruppe A pushed through the Ardennes in May 1940, they were not successful because of the brilliant thinking of senior Wehrmacht leaders. Rather, most of them opposed the very "sickle cut" plan developed by General Erich von Manstein. The reason for German success in France was due mostly to the ability of the leaders in the spearhead to press ahead without waiting on support from senior commanders, largely because they had the logistical independence to make such decisions.

When the Allies drove across France in 1944, US Army senior leaders had not envisioned the breakout and pursuit that occurred, even though their army had trained to conduct such an operation. Unlike their German counterparts, who received their initial knowledge of operational art from combat experience in the early months of the war, US Army divisions, corps, and armies trained at the operational level for several years prior to the campaign in France. While many students of World War II are familiar with the famous US Army Louisiana and North Carolina maneuvers of 1941, it is often overlooked that the US Army continued to train in this fashion up to early 1944, conducting large-scale operational maneuvers involving numerous divisions, higher headquarters, and hundreds of thousands of troops and vehicles.

Preparing soldiers for battle is much more than teaching them the essentials of weapons and tactics. Soldiers are initially trained individually, developing a set of basic skills. After this, soldiers are integrated into small formations, such as infantry squads, tank or gun crews, or support teams. Once they have mastered the essentials at this level, the process continues, with soldiers being trained as part of platoons, companies, and battalions. Each level integrates previously learned skillsets, and meshes them with ones demanded at higher levels of organization. For example, an artilleryman first learns basic soldier skills, such as shooting his personal weapon, maintaining his personal equipment, and the boring but very important aspect of field sanitation. From there, he becomes part of a gun crew, where he learns to fire and maintain the crew-served weapon. Afterwards, his crew is integrated with a battery, typically of four to six pieces of artillery, and later woven together with other batteries to form a battalion, and so on.

All of this appears mundane on the surface but is the very essence as to how combat units are developed. Units trained only at the platoon level will have a very difficult time integrating effectively in a company, and so forth up the ladder of command. If units do not train together, they will not understand each other and will thus be largely ineffective in combat environments that demand a large measure of maneuver, where confusion is rampant. Instead, they will be more comfortable in static defense. Since combat is one of the most confusing activities one can participate in, it is of critical importance that communication between units, often attempted in chaotic circumstances, must be as clear and precise as humanly possible. Sometimes communication must even be intuitive, almost as if by osmosis, when regular channels break down. Only extensive training and familiarity between soldiers can create such interaction. This issue of unit-level training cannot be underscored too firmly; failure regarding such higher-level integration of combat units is a significant factor in ultimate victory or defeat in combat.

Interestingly, the pre-World War II German Army engaged in only a few maneuvers that went beyond the divisional level, these being in 1932 and 1937. Otherwise, German units typically trained only up to the divisional level at best, and more commonly at regimental level. As the war dragged on, it rarely exceeded battalion level, and often was only up to company level. By limiting training to the regimental or battalion level, the Wehrmacht found itself focusing increasingly on tactics, thus ignoring the operational art except on map exercises. In contrast, US Army forces, by training at the operational level, began to focus more on that aspect, which was a boon particularly for staff officers, where logisticians and planners got a feel for real-world action in their specialties. By late 1944, US units may not have been as tactically capable as some German units, but operationally they were without peer, and hence this was a key ingredient for their success in the field.

For commanders and staff, there is nothing close to directing troops in the field; map exercises, while useful, are a mediocre substitute for the real thing. Unlike the genteel landscape of paper and unit markers, large-scale exercises cause everyone, from the soldier all the way to the senior commander, to experience a taste of the stress, confusion, and frustration of operations. Units get lost or fail to make their start time on a march, thus causing a ripple effect that impacts dozens of other units and hundreds of vehicles and thousands of men. Vehicles break down or get mired in mud, or collide with other vehicles due to driver fatigue. Supplies are misdirected or even stolen by other units. Communications break down, leaving senior commanders virtually in the dark. The weather turns, with sleet dashing into the faces of man and beast, and sending tanks to perform circles on icy roads. Soldiers curse, sergeants growl, and officers fume, with all never having a clear idea what is beyond the next terrain feature. Meanwhile, staff officers struggle through all the problems to gain experience and develop solutions, learning the true meaning of Carl von Clausewitz's use of the word "friction." None of this can be properly experienced on a game table.

After the first year in Russia, the Wehrmacht began to change

A pair of Jagdpanzer IV/70s, probably belonging to 2.Panzer-Division, abandoned near Hochscheid in mid-March. This vehicle mounted the effective 75mm L/70 gun, but was of marginal use on the attack due to its lack of a turret. Nevertheless, the Jagdpanzer IV/70 was cited in German reports as a "PzKpfw IV/70," being seen as a substitute for a tank. (US Army Signal Corps/The General George Patton Museum)

dramatically. The bold theorists of blitzkrieg, who had perfected their operational craft in the dash to the English Channel or during the massive pockets in the Ukraine, now found themselves squeezed ever tighter into the tactical straitjacket. German training emphasized tactics, tactics, and more tactics, in part caused by rising casualties at the front but also by the prevailing mindset among most senior German commanders that downplayed the importance of the operational level. When Manstein urged Hitler to give him more freedom of action on the Eastern Front in early 1944, he was asking for an operational level mandate to counter the growing numerical weight of Soviet forces. Hitler would have none of it and sacked him.

Staff work is often neglected in historical analysis, but staffs can make or break any operation. A good staff can make even a mediocre commander look brilliant. American staff work, despite the legends of the German General Staff system and its effectiveness, was superior to the Germans at the operational level. American corps and army staffs received extensive maneuver experience in handling real-world operations, which included both the long distance movement of forces and their supply. In contrast, German staffs were more experienced at handling tactical matters. Here, a typical Wehrmacht replacement unit staff handles day-to-day operations in Russia in 1944. The author's grandfather is on the phone. (Author's collection)

The record of new formations created during the war bear this out, with even some of the more elite like the 10.SS-Panzer-Division "Frundsberg" training only up to battalion level before being committed to action. It was because of the emphasis on tactics that German units, even into the last months of the war, were often tactically superior to Allied formations. Underscoring this focus on tactics was the Wehrmacht replacement system. Each division had its own replacement battalion, often deployed far in the rear of the front lines and composed of an experienced cadre, where new replacements received additional training and integration into a unit before being sent to the front. These battalions were considered so valuable that senior German leaders did everything they could to keep such assets out of combat, only relenting out of sheer necessity during the last months of the war. These factors, coupled with combat-seasoned, small-unit leaders, led to units that could fight well, especially in the defense.

This lack of operational-level training accomplished through large-scale maneuvers would have a telling impact on the Wehrmacht. This led to such decisions as squandering the German Panzer force through constant demands to perform tactical-level tasks. As a consequence, Panzer divisions increasingly found themselves broken up and scattered into small *Kampfgruppen* (battlegroups) to assist infantry units in resisting Red Army assaults and breakthroughs. Maneuver-oriented thinkers, like Guderian, would argue vehemently against such techniques, typically without success. Late in the war, the Wehrmacht did attempt to conduct several larger offensives, but if one examines such operations as *Wacht am Rhein* (Ardennes 1944), and *Frülingserwachen* (Hungary 1945), what the Germans committed to those operations was significantly less than what they deployed through the Ardennes in 1940. For example, Panzergruppe Kleist, the spearhead of the Ardennes attack in 1940, had 1,222 panzers; for *Frülingserwachen*, Heeresgruppe Süd could muster only 528 panzers. Moreover, the conduct of these late-war operations was sluggish and indecisive; the operational élan was gone.

As the US Army prepared its commanders and staffs to handle larger formations in the field, this bore fruit at the operational level. In fact, the emphasis on these larger maneuvers caused a neglect of small-unit tactical training that came to the notice of the highest levels of the army, where efforts were made to turn such circumstances around. Midway through the war, directives were issued to use more live ammunition during training, and to more aggressively train small-unit leaders for actual combat by emulating realistic conditions. Eventually, such training was integrated into the larger maneuvers to provide what the Army Ground Forces under Lieutenant-General Lesley McNair described as the "sight, sound, and sensation of battle."[2] Ironically, such instructions were issued like some prophetic oracle just a few weeks prior to the beating American forces would take at Kasserine.

Of the major exercises, those of 1943 are considered to have been the most extensive and beneficial. In the case of the February maneuvers in the Mojavi Desert, the plan called for the railroad movement of some units up to 2,400km. In contrast, the approximate straight-line distance from Warsaw, Poland to Moscow was just under 1,400km. This movement engaged the service forces in fully realistic supply operations, rather than relying on simulated loads. Therefore, while combat units sometimes still "pretended" to have tactical battle control, logistic and staff elements managed the real thing at the operational level, allowing staffs to hone procedures through practical experience. In addition, an incompetent officer, whether senior leader or staff member, might be identified and transferred, though there are notable exceptions when this did not happen, such as Major-General Lloyd Fredendall managing to slip through the sieve to later command the US II Corps during the debacle at Kasserine Pass in early 1943.

The British Army conducted similar large-scale exercises, but much smaller in number and scale of area to their American cousins. Exercise *Bumper*, conducted in the fall of 1941, involved two army headquarters, four corps, and 12 divisions, with three being armored, and was the largest exercise conducted in Britain. Exercise *Spartan*, conducted in the spring of 1943, involved ten divisions, a significant number being Canadian. Besides exercising staffs, these training events convinced senior British leaders, like Lord Alanbrooke, that the commander of the Canadian First Army, Lieutenant-General Andrew McNaughton, was not competent for such senior responsibility. He would be replaced later by General Henry Crerar, who would prove himself to be one of the outstanding combat leaders of the war.

Staff procedures are almost never written about in history books. The work is considered boring in contrast to combat operations, and yet it is the staff work that often brings success or failure in battle. A typical army headquarters could number from 350 to 500 or more officers and enlisted personnel, and because of this number many do not know

One of the secrets of American success was a carefully prepared and executed plan of artillery support. By early 1945, even towed guns were essentially motorized, drawn by what were called "high-speed tractors" like this 38-ton M6 tractor towing a 240mm howitzer on March 25 in support of the Oppenheim crossing. The US Army was innovative in developing artillery support, and it was Lieutenant-General Jacob Devers, in his previous role as the commander of the Artillery School at Fort Sill, Oklahoma who developed the methods of calling for artillery support that are still used by the US Army today. (NARA)

one another unless they get opportunities to work extensively together. J.F.C. Fuller once wrote that the purpose of a staff is to relieve a commander of work, but this is only part of it. The staff not only is the commander's arms and legs to the units in the field, but it also recommends courses of action to be followed. Staff officers collect, sift, and evaluate large quantities of information in an effort to bring a measure of clarity to the confusion of war. Moreover, they plan both operations and logistical support to bring those plans to successful fruition. In day-to-day operations, staff officers who know one another can find the most rapid and effective means to accomplish the tasks at hand. Inexperienced staff, or those who are strangers to each other, will be inefficient and marginally effective.

The US Army's operational training program, especially that in 1943 and into 1944, was the most effective of such programs instituted by any of the belligerents during World War II. The experience gained paid handsome dividends, especially for the combat units engaged in the European Theater of Operations, and particularly for a combat force driven by the personality of Patton. Moreover, the training received was enhanced by operational success in 1944 when American forces pushed across France. It also paid off when Patton had to rotate the lion's share of his army 90 degrees to the north to slash into the flank of the German Ardennes counteroffensive. Patton's assistant G-2, Colonel Robert Allen, may have praised the spirit of the Third US Army for such feats, but the training program they had endured deserves much of the credit. Patton's drive through the Palatinate and his crossing of the Rhine is as much a testimony of the efforts of his staff as it is to the gallantry of the first men who muddied their boots on the east bank of that great water barrier.

In contrast, the Wehrmacht was not only a shadow of its former self, but had nothing close to the operational training program of its American counterparts. After the 1937 maneuvers, German forces gained their operational training through actual experience, such as the occupation of the Sudetenland and Czechoslovakia, as well as the invasion of Poland. It was in these operations that staff officers at the corps and army level were able to obtain valuable know-how in moving large numbers of troops. Otherwise, their operational training was on a map. Even preparation for the campaign against France in 1940 saw the Panzer force sit largely idle, in large measure to maintain secrecy of the coming sickle cut through the Ardennes. Rather than conduct real maneuvers, German planners had to be satisfied with map exercises. As the war progressed, their emphasis on tactics led to the neglect of mobile operations, exacerbated by an increasingly desperate fuel shortage that plagued the entire Wehrmacht and allowed the Allies to gain mastery of the skies.

Losses in both materiel and manpower also forced the German leadership to repeatedly reorganize their army. Efforts were taken to use more advanced technologies as a combat substitute for soldiers in the field, and this covered every aspect of the German war machine. New small arms, tanks, assault guns, and aircraft were pushed forward, but typically too little, too late. Germany had not mastered

The desperation within the German military machine can be amply seen by illustrations that show trained soldiers trying to provide crash courses to civilians on how to fight tanks with weapons like magnetic antitank mines. Combat soldiers engaged in extensive training to fight tanks, and to expect civilians to overcome "tank fear" was something from what many Germans would consider to be a *Wolkenkuckucksheim* (cloud cuckoo land). (Bundesarchiv, Bild 146-1971-033-09)

the techniques of vehicle mass production like the United States, as they continued to build tanks and aircraft as a form of artistic craft rather than on moving assembly lines. Even as they built hundreds of a new tank, their opponents manufactured thousands of a proven design. Divisions were reorganized multiple times in just a few years so as to reduce their manpower while trying to increase their firepower, yet could never produce sufficient equipment to compensate for this loss in manpower. German leaders quickly discovered that firepower

was not enough; they still needed human beings to physically occupy critical positions. And with the inability of industry to produce the necessary motor transport and fuel to increase tactical maneuverability, German units found themselves defending increasingly large combat frontages with their rapidly dwindling forces dug into static positions.

German infantry positioned near Trier with a 50mm PAK. Despite obsolescence, many weapons like the 50mm antitank gun, and even 37mm guns, were pressed into service due to dire need. Despite the increase in armaments production under Reichsminister Speer, the German war machine could not produce enough equipment to replace heavy losses, with much of the equipment abandoned out of necessity when infantry units were overrun by more mobile enemy units. (Bundesarchiv, Bild 101I-497-3518-31)

The contrast between Germany and the United States can be seen most dramatically in the production of trucks and aircraft. Germany built just over 347,000 trucks of all types. In contrast, the United States sent 357,000 Lend-Lease trucks to the Soviet Union alone, not counting ¼-ton jeeps. Overall, the Americans built a staggering 2,300,000 trucks. There is a good reason why Patton said that the American 2½-ton truck, the famous "Deuce-and-a-half," was the weapon that won World War II. Regarding aircraft, the Germans produced just over 110,000 planes of all types, compared to the again staggering number of 265,000 produced by the United States. In essence, the Germans built equipment in dribs and drabs, while the United States flooded the world with machines of all types.

By early 1945, German divisions had been reorganized to near extinction compared to their early war counterparts. The Panzer divisions had been organizationally slashed to a single Panzer battalion with 40 tanks, and at that late date were fortunate to actually have that many on hand. A number of the infantry divisions had been transformed to the Volksgrenadier organization, which cut its motorization by over half from its early war predecessor. This, along with the fuel shortages, ensured that the German infantry would be only useful in prepared, static defensive positions.

In contrast, a US infantry division had over 700 trucks, excluding jeeps. Moreover, American army commands could draw upon well-equipped centralized pools of trucks to motorize entire divisions if necessary. Indeed, one of Patton's well-used techniques was to motorize an infantry regiment and attach it to one of his armored divisions for exploitation purposes, drawing trucks from the 42 truck companies organic to his command. For the Germans, horse-drawn carts to move equipment and supplies were a poor substitute in an era of machine warfare. Once a defensive line was compromised, a virtual rout would ensue if the enemy were exceptionally mobile. When Hitler's infamous "no retreat" orders were added to the mix, the disasters that would ensue were readily apparent.

German field commanders had a ready appreciation for these dilemmas and took measures to compensate as best they could. To blunt Hitler's orders, many of them exercised a technique by which they kept a front line thinly manned with what could best be described as a screen, while the main body of men were significantly further back, often by 20km or more, in a supplemental defensive position. They did this without informing higher headquarters, and thus the OKW would often be deceived as to the true nature of the situation. While believing that a forward position was firmly held, the field commanders had long ago all but abandoned it. Nevertheless, such disobedience to Hitler's orders was only partially successful and practiced mostly in the West, where field commanders were hesitant to employ flying tribunals to summarily execute soldiers deemed to be deserters.

By early 1945, the Wehrmacht suffered one catastrophe after another. A line would be penetrated by enemies both east and west and the infantry units would be overrun and destroyed. In this manner, the already critical shortages were made worse with repeated heavy losses in both men and materiel. For example, when the Soviets launched their Vistula–Oder Offensive on January 12, 1945, Heeresgruppe A under Generaloberst Joseph Harpe disintegrated, losing well over 400,000 killed, wounded, and prisoners, not to mention the loss of rifles, artillery pieces, signal equipment, and trucks. The OKW continued to reorganize and pour every living soul it could muster into the army. Many naval and aviation personnel were sifted from their organizations and sent as replacements for the devastated infantry units. This raw material of humanity was able to bring many units reasonably close to authorized strength at any given time, but they were no substitute for combat-trained soldiers well integrated into divisions and corps.

Elements of the 11th Armored Division cross the Nahe River south of Kirn. The vehicle on the bridge is a ¾-ton Dodge often used for special weapons units, while the truck in the river is a 2½-ton truck, the famous "Deuce-and-a-half" that was the backbone of Allied motorization. Between the GMC and Studebaker models, the US built close to 800,000 of these vehicles, dwarfing German truck production. Patton was not exaggerating when he commented that the Deuce-and-a-half was the weapon that won the war. (NARA)

Many German civilians were press-ganged by the military to dig antitank trenches and other fortifications. Those particularly targeted for these tasks were those whom local Nazi party officials deemed to be troublemakers or uncooperative with the regime. (Bundesarchiv, Bild 101I-590-2332-26)

ORDERS OF BATTLE

The tables below demonstrate the ebb and flow of units for both sides.

GERMAN

7.ARMEE (GENERAL DER INFANTERIE HANS FELBER; FROM MARCH 25, GENERAL DER INFANTERIE HANS VON OBSTFELDER)

7.Armee

Subunit	March 13	March 20	March 22	March 25
LXXXIX.Armee-Korps (General der Infanterie Gustav Höhne)	Kampfgruppe Koblenz; Kampfgruppe 276. Volksgrenadier-Division; 159. Volksgrenadier-Division; Elements of 6.SS-Gebirgs-Division "Nord"	To Heeresgruppe B		
XIII.Armee-Korps (Generalluetnant Ralph Graf von Oriola)	Kampfgruppe Wilke; 9. Volksgrenadier-Division; 2.Panzer-Division; 246. Volksgrenadier-Division	Temporary addition of 47.Volksgrenadier-Division (then to 1.Armee); Added 559.Volksgrenadier-Division	2.Panzer-Division remnants; 246.Volksgrenadier-Division remnants; 352.Volksgrenadier-Division remnants; 559. Volksgrenadier-Division remnants; 553.Grenadier-Division remnants; 17.SS-Panzer-Grenadier-Division (reforming)	Loses 246. Volksgrenadier-Division; No combat power at this point.
LXXX.Armee-Korps (General der Infanterie Franz Beyer)	352.Volksgrenadier-Division; 212.Volksgrenadier-Division; Kampfgruppe 79.Volksgrenadier-Division	To 1.Armee		
XII.Armee-Korps (prov.), (Wehrkreis XII) (General der Infanterie Herbert Osterkamp)			159.Volksgrenadier-Division remnants; Kampfgruppe Frankfurt; General Kurt von Berg's Division (North); General Siegfried Runge's Division (Central); General Konrad von Alberti's Division (South); Reserve Officer's Candidate School force, Oberst Gerhard Kentner	Added Division Nr. 413; Added 246. Volksgrenadier-Division; Loses General Siegfried Runge's Division; Loses Kampfgruppe Frankfurt
LXXXV.Armee-Korps (General der Infanterie Baptist Kniess)			Added Frankfrut area after March 22	Elements of 6.SS-Gebirgs-Division "Nord"; 198.Infanterie-Division; Added Kampfgruppe Frankfurt

1.ARMEE (GENERAL DER INFANTERIE HERMANN FÖRTSCH)

1.Armee

Subunit	March 15	March 22
LXXXII.Armee-Korps (General Walther Hahm)	Kampfgruppe 79.Volksgrenadier-Division; SS-Gebirgsjäger-Regiment 12, 6.SS-Gebirgs-Division "Nord"; 2.Gebirgs-Division; 416. Infanterie-Division	
LXXXV.Armee-Korps (General der Infanterie Baptist Kniess)	347.Infanterie-Division; 719.Infanterie-Division	HQ transferred to Frankfurt area
XIII.SS-Armee-Korps (SS-Gruppenführer Max Simon)	16.Volksgrenadier-Division; 19.Volksgrenadier-Division; 17.SS-Panzergrenadier-Division	
XC.Armee-Korps (General der Infanterie Erich Petersen)	36.Volksgrenadier-Division; 257. Volksgrenadier-Division; Division Nr. 905	

LUFTWAFFE[3]

Luftwaffenkommando West (Generalleutnant Joseph "Beppo" Schmid)

(Formerly Luftflotte 3; supported western Germany and Netherlands; approximately 127 serviceable of all types, April 9, 1945; in repair 97—total 224)

Kampfgeschwader 51

    I.Gruppe (Me 262); based at Giebelstadt March 20, south of Würzburg; moved to Leipheim by Ulm on March 30; by April 21 in Memmingen.

    II.Gruppe (Me 262); based at Schwäbisch Hall on March 21, then Fürth March 30, and Linz in April.

    III.Gruppe (probably Me 410)

    IV.Gruppe (probably Me 410)

Kampfgeschwader 54—part of Luftflotte Reich; approximately 35 Me 262; based in Zerbst and Kitzingen and Erding.

Other available forces

Luftflotte Reich (Generaloberst Hans-Jürgen Stumpf)

(Supported Greater Germany against Allied strategic air offensive. In January 1945, Luftflotte Reich had 389 serviceable fighters, with just over 100 being Me 262s, and there were 485 night fighters available. Fuel shortages limited actual deployment. At April 9, 1945, it had approximately 952 serviceable of all types, with 429 in repair—for a grand total of 1,381.)

Jagdgeschwader 2 (Fw 190); 16 serviceable

Jagdgeschwader 4 (Fw 190 and Bf 109); 94 serviceable

Jagdgeschwader 7 (Me 262); 53 serviceable

Jagdgeschwader 26 (Fw 190); 63 serviceable

Jagdgeschwader 27 (Bf 109); 55 serviceable

Kampfgeschwader 54 (Me 262); 21 serviceable

Jagdgeschwader 301 (Ta 152 and Fw 190); 41 serviceable

Jagdgeschwader 400 (Me 163); 22 serviceable

Jagdgruppe 10 (Fw 190); 9 serviceable

Jagdverband 44 (Me 262); 15 serviceable

Nachtjagdgeschwader 1 (He 219/Bf 110); 88 serviceable

Nachtjagdgeschwader 2 (Ju 88); 62 serviceable

Nachtjagdgeschwader 3 (Ju 88); 49 serviceable

Nachtjagdgeschwader 4 (Ju 88/Bf 110); 47 serviceable

Nachtjagdgeschwader 5 (Ju 88/Bf 110/He 219); 88 serviceable

Nachtjagdgeschwader 6 (Ju 88/Bf 110); 65 serviceable

Nachtjagdgeschwader 11 (Bf 109/Me 262); 50 serviceable

Nachtjagdgeschwader 100 (Ju 88/Fw 58); 20 serviceable

Kommando Bonow (Ar 234); 1 serviceable

Nachtschlachtgruppe 1 (Ju 87); 1 serviceable

Nachtschlachtgruppe 2 (Ju 87); 5 serviceable

Nachtschlachtgruppe 20 (Fw 190); 11 serviceable

Nahaufklärungsgruppe 1 (Bf 109); 9 serviceable

Nahaufklärungsgruppe 6 (Me 262); 3 serviceable

Nahaufklärungsgruppe 14 (Fw 189); 4 serviceable

Kampfgeschwader 200 (Ju 188/Fw 190/Mistel Ju 88/transports); 60 serviceable

Luftwaffenkommando West

Jagdgeschwader 53 (Bf 109); 76 serviceable (dedicated to Heeresgruppe G January–March 1945)

Kampfgeschwader 51 (Me 262); 13 serviceable

Kampfgeschwader 76 (Ar 234); 4 serviceable

Fernaufklärungsgruppe 100 (Ar 234); 1 serviceable

Fernaufklärungsgruppe 123 (Ar 234/Ju 188); 7 serviceable

Nahaufklärungsgruppe 13 (Bf 109); 26 serviceable

Other commands

Luftwaffenkommando Courland (formerly Luftflotte 1); supported Courland Pocket

Luftwaffe General Italy (formerly Luftflotte 2); located in northern Italy

Luftflotte 4; located in Austria/Hungary/the Balkans

Luftwaffe General Norway (formerly Luftflotte 5); supported Norway and Finland

Luftflotte 6: Eastern Front on the Oder River and Czechoslovakian front

Glossary

Jagdgeschwader	fighter squadron
Kampfgeschwader	ground attack squadron
Jagdgruppe	fighter group
Jagdverband	fighter formation
Nachtjagdgeschwader	night fighter squadron
Nachtschlachtgruppe	night attack group
Nahaufklärungsgruppe	short range tactical reconnaissance
Fernaufklärungsgruppe	long range reconnaissance

3   Sources:
Maurer, Maurer, *Combat Squadrons of the Air Force, World War II*, Washington, DC: Office of Air Force History, 1982
McNab, Chris, *German Luftwaffe in World War II: Order of Battle*, London: Amber Books, 2009
Office of Statistical Control, *Army Air Forces Statistical Digest, World War II*, 1945
Price, Alfred, *The Luftwaffe Data Book*, London: Greenhill Books, 1997
USAF Historical Division Liaison Office, *USAF Tactical Operations, World War II and Korea*, 1962
XIX Tactical Air Command Report, *Tactical Air Operations in Europe*, 1945

US

THIRD US ARMY (LIEUTENANT-GENERAL GEORGE S. PATTON)

Third US Army

Unit	March 13	March 17	March 20	March 22 (total list)	March 25
VIII Corps (Major-General Troy H. Middleton)	6th Cavalry Group; 11th Armored Division; 87th Infantry Division	Loses 11th Armored Division; added 28th Infantry Division	Added 76th Infantry Division	6th Cavalry Group; 76th Infantry Division; 87th Infantry Division; 89th Infantry Division	
XII Corps (Major-General Manton S. Eddy)	2nd Cavalry Group; 4th Armored Division; 5th Infantry Division; 76th Infantry Division; 89th Infantry Division; 90th Infantry Division	Added 11th Armored Division	Loses 76th Infantry Division	2nd Cavalry Group; 4th Armored Division; 11th Armored Division; 5th Infantry Division; 26th Infantry Division; 90th Infantry Division	Added 16th Cavalry Group and 6th Armored Division; loses 11th Armored Division
XX Corps (Major-General Walton Walker)	3rd Cavalry Group; 10th Armored Division; 26th Infantry Division; 65th Infantry Division; 80th Infantry Division; 94th Infantry Division	Added 12th Armored Division and 16th Cavalry Group		3rd Cavalry Group; 10th Armored Division; 12th Armored Division; 65th Infantry Division; 80th Infantry Division; 94th Infantry Division	Added 11th Armored Division; loses 10th Armored Division and 12th Armored Division

SEVENTH US ARMY (LIEUTENANT-GENERAL ALEXANDER PATCH)

Seventh US Army

Unit	March 15	March 21	March 22
XXI Corps (Major-General Frank W. Milburn)	63rd Infantry Division; 70th Infantry Division	Loses 63rd Infantry Division	Added 71st Infantry Division and 100th Infantry Division
XV Corps (Major-General Wade H. Haislip)	106th Cavalry Group; 6th Armored Division; 3th Infantry Division; 44th Infantry Division; 45th Infantry Division; 71st Infantry Division; 100th Infantry Division	Loses 44th Infantry Division (March 16); added 63rd Infantry Division	Loses 71st Infantry Division and 100th Infantry Division
VI Corps (Major-General Edward H. Brooks)	14th Armored Division; 3rd Algerian Infantry Division; 36th Infantry Division; 42nd Infantry Division; 103rd Infantry Division		

To the Rhine and Moselle, February 8–March 12, 1945

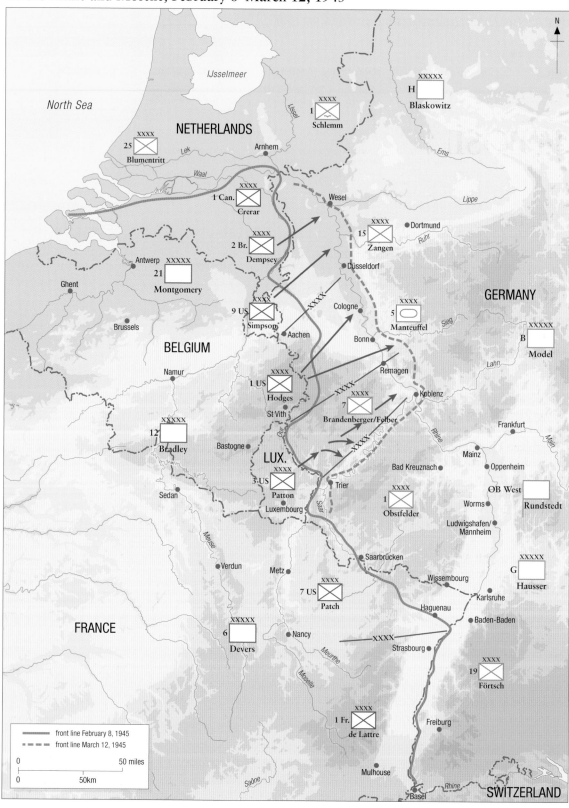

OPPOSING PLANS

GERMAN

By early March 1945, the German forces in the central portion of the Western Front were falling back toward the Moselle River. These forces, now under the command of Heeresgruppe G commanded by SS-Oberst-Gruppenführer Paul Hausser, were still ordered to hold the Siegfried Line, and true to form a screen was deployed along most of the line to provide this illusion. An exception was the area around Trier and the Saar, where German units continued to fight fiercely for the ancient city and the critical industrial region near Saarbrücken, even as units to the north fled as quickly as their legs could carry them to the Moselle. Two of Heeresgruppe G's best divisions, 6.SS-Gebirgs-Division "Nord" and 17.SS-Panzergrenadier-Division "Götz von Berlichingen," were tied up trying to save Trier and the Saar respectively. Regarding Trier, the demand to save the city was so firm that one of the two Jagdtiger units, schwere Panzerjäger-Abteilung 653 with 41 of the super-heavy tank destroyers, was deployed in the area. This single unit represented at least one-fifth of the entire armor support available to Heeresgruppe G, and the coming battle would demonstrate that it was deployed to the wrong area.

When Trier fell to Patton's 10th Armored Division on March 2, 6.SS-Gebirgs-Division was ordered to counterattack and sever the supply line into the city. Despite having initial success and temporarily isolating the city, the weight of the 10th Armored and 94th Infantry divisions stopped this attack and turned the hunter into the prey. 6.SS-Gebirgs-Division was forced to fall back, leaving one of its two regiments, SS-Gebirgsjäger Regiment 12, to continue the fight. The remainder, comprising SS-Gebirgsjäger Regiment 11 and the reconnaissance battalion, received orders to redeploy to the Koblenz area.

Meanwhile, 17.SS-Panzergrenadier-Division was busy fighting south of Zweibrücken in and out of the fortifications of the Siegfried Line. Their losses had been so heavy that on March 5, the division commander, SS-Standartenführer Fritz Klingenberg, ordered that the service units of the division be stripped of personnel to flesh out the infantry formations. By March 16, the division had withdrawn fully into the Siegfried Line fortifications.

As the German forces on the Western Front fell back, those to the north of Koblenz and south of Wissembourg, France had retreated to the east bank of the Rhine. But it was in the center, an area known as the Saar-Palatinate Triangle, where two armies protruded westward as they continued to cling to portions of the Siegfried Line. On the southern shoulder of this wedge-

While the Panther tank is often cited as the best tank of the war, it had an abysmal maintenance record and low readiness rates when compared to its more robust opponents like the American M4 Sherman and Soviet T-34. The tank's teething troubles strained the already overtaxed German logistical system, problems that were only partially fixed by later versions. By 1945, few Panthers were available to face Patton's army, with but around 100 operational vehicles concentrated in the north near the Ruhr industrial district. (US Army Signal Corps/The General George Patton Museum)

like salient stood 1.Armee under General Hermann Förtsch. He had taken command of the army on February 28 after he and General Hans von Obstfelder swapped roles, with the latter taking command of 19.Armee further south. The 1.Armee held a line that extended from Trier to the Rhine in the area of northern Alsace-Lorraine, just south of the Franco-German border. While covering a considerable distance, the terrain defended was more rugged and Förtsch's army was in reasonably good shape.

On the north shoulder of this bulge was General Hans Felber's 7.Armee. The latter had been assigned to the southern edge of the German Ardennes Offensive in December and had then been commanded by General Erich Brandenberger. The army had suffered significant losses in its withdrawal from the Ardennes and the subsequent pounding it took along the Siegfried Line. When it set up defensive positions along the Moselle River, its task was to protect the northern flank of 1.Armee, but was considerably weaker.

Felber's command was assigned three corps, but they were in name only. On the right flank, anchored on the confluence of the Moselle and Rhine rivers at Koblenz, was General Gustav Höhne's LXXXIX.Armee-Korps. His corps held positions along the Moselle southwest to the picturesque town of Cochem. He had a 1,800-man *Kampfgruppe* in Koblenz under Oberstleutnant Ernst Löffler, the staff of the decimated 276.Volksgrenadier-Division, the rebuilt 159.Volksgrenadier-Division, and an assortment of antiaircraft, ad hoc "alarm" units, and Volksturm. The 276.Volksgrenadier-Division, led by Oberst Werner Wagner controlled most of the fragments sent to the area, and in mid-March the reconnaissance battalion of 6.SS-Gebirgs-Division "Nord" was just moving into Höhne's sector near Koblenz.

The centerpiece of Höhne's defensive line was 159.Volksgrenadier-Division, under the command of Generalmajor Heinrich Bürcky. The division had been originally organized in September 1939 to serve as a replacement and training unit, and by October 1942, it had been renamed a reserve division when the Wehrmacht reorganized its replacement structure. Its primary job was to train new units for deployment at the front and to engage in occupation duties in southwest France. The Allied invasion of France shattered this tranquil existence, forcing the division to be thrown into combat. After taking serious losses, the division was rebuilt as a Volksgrenadier formation, but its training was cut short, being ordered—notwithstanding Bürcky's protests—to join LXXXIX.Armee-Korps on the Moselle. In one of those strange twists of history, this nondescript unit would play a central though ultimately unsuccessful part in the coming campaign.

To the left of Höhne's corps stood XIII.Armee-Korps under Generalluetnant Ralph Graf von Oriola. During the withdrawal to the Moselle, he had managed to save all of his artillery, even though he lost most of his motor transport due to lack of fuel. His units were otherwise in bad shape. In Cochem, Oriola had a battlegroup formed from a mix of service units and Luftwaffe personnel under the nominal command of

Generalmajor der Luftwaffe Karl-Eduard Wilke, who was still in command of the 15.Flieger-Division based at Flammersfeld. The 15.Flieger-Division was assigned to provide what little air support was available to the middle Rhine front, and while bearing his name, it is unlikely that Wilke exercised command of "Division Wilke." This unit held the town of Cochem as a bridgehead on the west side of the Moselle.

From Cochem to the southwest was 9.Volksgrenadier-Division under Generalmajor der Reserve Werner Kolb, followed by 2.Panzer-Division under newly promoted Generalmajor Meinrad von Lauchert. The latter had a well-established reputation as a panzer leader, having commanded 2.Panzer-Division during the Ardennes Offensive. Prior to this, he had commanded Panzer-Brigade 101, and in 1943 had been tasked with organizing the first two PzKpfw V Panther battalions, which he then led during the Kursk Offensive. To the left of Lauchert's division was 246.Volksgrenadier-Division under Generalmajor Walter Kühn, which held the river to the town of Mülheim, a point just west of Bernkastel. All of these divisions were a mere shadow of their former selves, and even 2.Panzer-Division was a skeleton, having fewer than two dozen tanks and assault guns on hand. This division should have been in reserve, but there was simply too much front to cover and therefore was forced into the line.

Rounding out 7.Armee was General Franz Beyer's LXXX.Armee-Korps, which was assigned to cover the Moselle from west of Mülheim to the outskirts of Trier. The 352.Volksgrenadier-Division, famous for its stand at Omaha Beach on June 6, 1944, and commanded by Generalmajor der Reserve Rudolph von Oppen, had just taken up positions along the river from Mülheim to Reinsport. It had absorbed some of the remnants of 560.Volksgrenadier-Division, whose headquarters had been withdrawn for refitting. This was followed by 212. Volksgrenadier-Division, led by Generalleutnant Franz Sensfuss, which held the line to Mehring. And on the far left of Beyer's front in what was called the Ruwer sector was the *Kampfgruppe* of 79.Volksgrenadier-Division, at that time ably led by Oberstleutnant Cord von Hobe. This unit had fought fiercely to help defend Trier, but had now pulled back to defend along the valley of the Feller stream just east of the city. Because of the nebulous nature of the area, Hobe's unit would find itself assigned back and forth between Beyer's corps and that of his left-hand neighbor, the LXXXII.Armee-Korps of 1.Armee. Beyer's units were in much the same condition as Oriola's, with 212.Volksgrenadier-Division his strongest formation.

Regarding armor, it would seem that 7.Armee had no more than 80 tanks and assault guns, which would be close to the estimate provided by Patton's G-2. But while Patton's intelligence personnel estimated the German force to be the equivalent of about two-and-a-half divisions, by March 15 it would be close to five division equivalents with the inclusion of Höhne's corps into the line.

The orders from Hitler and OKW was for Heeresgruppe G and its subordinate armies to hold as long as possible with the

Indicative of the dissolution of the German war machine was the fate of General Meinrad von Lauchert, who commanded the famous 2.Panzer-Division. As the US 4th Armored Division drove deep into the rear areas of 7.Armee, he was ordered to launch a counterattack with but six armored vehicles and 200 infantry. Soon disgusted with the war, Lauchert deserted and walked home. (Bundesarchiv, Bild 146-1973-005-16)

promise that new units and new "wonder weapons" were forthcoming. While seemingly nonsense on the surface, German commanders were hampered by Führer Order No. 1 of January 13, 1940, which stipulated that no commander should know more than was absolutely essential for him to accomplish the given mission for his command. As a consequence, senior officers operated in a vacuum, not truly aware of what was happening on other fronts other than generalities. In addition, Hitler increasingly involved himself in some of the most incredible minutia of day-to-day operations, tying the hands of his field commanders to the point that they were no more than action officers for his will. Nevertheless, Hausser and his subordinate commanders had at least made modest plans to abandon the Saar-Palatinate Triangle if things got too rough, even if they had to go around Hitler's directives.

US

Opposing 7.Armee was Patton's Third US Army. While organizationally about the same size as his German counterpart, Patton's units were not only at full strength but were manned by combat-seasoned veterans with experienced commanders and staffs. Furthermore, Third US Army was much more mobile than the German units it faced. Patton had three corps at his disposal, but by March 12 had concentrated most of his forces in two of them. On the left was VIII Corps, commanded by Major-General Troy Middleton, assigned the task of clearing Koblenz and screening the area in the immediate vicinity of the confluence of the Moselle and Rhine rivers known fittingly as the Rhine–Moselle Triangle. Middleton had only the 87th Infantry Division, led by Major-General Frank Culin, Jr., and the 6th Cavalry Group. The 4th Infantry and 11th Armored divisions had been assigned to VIII Corps, but had just been pulled out of the line, with the former en route to reinforce the Seventh US Army and the latter placed in reserve as part of Patton's planned exploitation. The 11th was commanded by Brigadier-General Charles "Rattlesnake" Kilburn, though at that time Patton was not too happy with his performance and would soon relieve him, replacing him with Brigadier-General Holmes E. Dager.

To the southwest of VIII Corps was Major-General Manton S. Eddy's XII Corps, which constituted the prime striking force of Third US Army. The

Tanks from the 735th Tank Battalion, 87th Infantry Division prepare to be ferried across the Moselle River at Kobern in support of the 347th Infantry Regiment. A smoke screen has been deployed to help conceal the crossing. The 87th Division had been tasked to clear the Rhine–Moselle Triangle and the city of Koblenz, the latter defended by a German *Kampfgruppe* of 1,800 men under Oberstleutnant Erich Löffler. Despite Löffler's reputation as a tough combatant, Koblenz was held for only two days. (NARA)

90th Infantry Division, under the leadership of Major-General Herbert Earnest, was on the left side of the corps' sector. Earnest had just taken over command on March 2, replacing Major-General Lowell Rooks, who had moved on to be the Deputy of Operations (G-3) at Supreme Headquarters Allied Expeditionary Force (SHAEF). On the right was Major-General Leroy Irwin's 5th Infantry Division. Irwin and his team were already old hands at river crossing operations, so they did not anticipate much trouble with the Moselle. To the right of Irwin's division was the 89th Infantry Division, commanded by Major-General Thomas Finley. His current task was to clear out German bridgeheads south of Cochem. Further up the

Moselle and opposite the Bernkastel area was the 76th Infantry Division, under Major-General William Schmidt, patrolling the riverbank and also clearing out any nests of resistance. Both the 89th and 76th Infantry divisions were new to the front, with the 89th having just entered the line on March 12. Waiting in reserve was the 4th Armored Division under Major-General Hugh Gaffey, who had been Patton's chief of staff before assuming command of the division in early December 1944. The 4th Armored was arguably the best and most elite of the American armored formations in the European Theater of Operations, with its tank battalions having some of the highest kill-to-loss ratios of any tank formation against German armor. It was Eddy's corps that would carry the brunt of Patton's planned offensive.

Any kind of amphibious operation presented dangers beyond enemy action, one of the most obvious being drowning. Soldiers were often issued life preserver belts, but many did not wear them. Such risk-tasking was exacerbated by the tendency to often overload boats and amphibious trucks, which might then swamp or capsize. This soldier is being given oxygen after being pulled from the Rhine during the Boppard crossing on March 27. (NARA)

Further southeast of Bernkastel and on the right was Patton's third corps— XX Corps, led by Major-General Walton Walker, who was considered by Patton to be one of his most aggressive corps commanders. The 10th Armored Division under Major-General William Morris was on the left, resting in a forward assembly area. Like Kilburn, Patton was not pleased with Morris' performance, but neither he nor Walker could think of an adequate replacement for him. One of the incidents that soured Patton's opinion was when Morris lost contact with his bridge train prior to crossing the Saar River on February 22, thus stalling his attack. Patton ordered Morris to fine the officer in charge of the bridging unit, though in his diary Patton blamed not only Morris, but also Walker and himself, largely for not ensuring Morris could handle the missions assigned to him. The next day, during a press conference, Patton explained that the train had been "knocked out," demonstrating his unique characteristic of absorbing blameworthy acts into the milieu of the fortunes of war and thus protecting the public reputation of his subordinates, a pattern he continued in his postwar memoir *War as I Knew It*.

Walker's position continued south of Trier, with the 94th Infantry Division, commanded by Major-General Harry Malony just outside the city. It was Malony's men, fairly new to the front, who had absorbed the 6.SS-Gebirgs-Division's earlier attack. On Malony's right was the 80th Infantry Division, a seasoned formation under Major-General Horace McBride. On his immediate right was the 26th Infantry Division under Major-General Willard Paul. The 26th had already seen some action in eastern France, and the guiding hand of Paul had corrected some deficiencies to the point that Patton considered it to be one of the best divisions in his army. On the far right of the Third US Army was the 65th Infantry Division, a green unit under the command of Major-General Stanley Reinhart.

Thus, on the eve of the Third Army's offensive, Patton had nine infantry and three armored divisions poised to strike. Yet, Patton had several difficult "political" problems that threatened his plans. The first involved a new creation of Eisenhower's staff called the SHAEF Reserve. This "toy," as Patton dubbed it, was a direct outgrowth of the embarrassment that the Supreme Commander had felt when caught by surprise without a strategic reserve during the German Ardennes Offensive. It was a rotational force, and each time a commander received a division from the Reserve, he had to give one up. When Patton received the 10th Armored for his drive on Trier, he was faced with the real possibility that he would have to give up another to take its place. Indeed, by March 4 Patton was obliged to release the 6th Armored to this reserve.

Another threat to Patton's designs was the development by the Supreme Commander of what was called "The Plan," more officially known as SCAF (Supreme Command Allied Forces) 180. In essence, this was the decision to have the main thrust across the Rhine, and thus into the heart of Germany, made by Field Marshal Bernard Montgomery's 21st Army Group. Montgomery's command had been assembling along the Lower Rhine with the intent of crossing to the north of the Ruhr industrial district. According to "The Plan," the British formations were to be supported by the Ninth US Army under General William H. Simpson. Moreover, Montgomery wanted even more support, and demanded an additional ten divisions from Bradley's 12th US Army Group, essentially being the lion's share of the First US Army. Eisenhower told Montgomery that if these divisions were sent to support his Rhine crossing, then Bradley would command both the First and Ninth US Armies. Bradley sensed that Montgomery did not want to share any glory and the field marshal ultimately dropped his request.

Nevertheless, "The Plan" continued to exert a tremendous influence on decision making in the field. When Hodges' First US Army captured the Remagen Bridge intact on March 7, Major-General Harold "Pinky" Bull, the Operations Chief (G-3) at SHAEF came to see Bradley, chiding him that the bridge just was not in "The Plan." Bradley scowled and retorted, "What in hell do you want us to do, pull back and blow it up?" (Bradley 1999, p. 510). Bull moderated his stance, but still insisted that it was a needless complication, especially as he wanted three divisions from Bradley to support Lieutenant-General Jacob Devers' 6th US Army Group along the Upper Rhine. Bradley at last agreed to the transfer, but his tolerance for such interference had waned significantly.

During most of the campaign across France, Bradley had been fairly acquiescent to siding with Eisenhower when he made compromises that benefited Montgomery. But the subordination of Hodges' First US Army to Montgomery during the Ardennes Offensive had been taken by Bradley as a serious insult, and he began to side increasingly with Patton's opinions regarding operational decisions. With the incessant demands of the British field marshal for increasing support, Bradley and Patton both saw the need to keep their forces engaged with the enemy so as to provide adequate grounds to refuse such demands. The mere mention of Montgomery was enough to push Patton along to launch his attack across the Moselle and into the Palatinate as quickly as possible. And while he was to coordinate his offensive with that of Devers to his south, Patton decided not to wait as he viewed speed and surprise to be more crucial at this point than coordination. In Patton's mind, there was no doubt that the Wehrmacht had at last been whipped and the final triumph was at hand—and Patton was determined to be the one to complete this triumph.

While taken in the Ninth US Army sector near Seveln, Germany, this photo illustrates the stockpiling of bridging equipment in rear areas waiting to be called upon for deployment to a crossing site. Patton's staff did a far more effective job in planning and moving such equipment to the front than most of his counterparts. In both the Moselle and Rhine crossings, he had bridges built within one day, whereas Hodges' First US Army at Remagen relied upon the Ludendorff Bridge for four days before completing a second bridge. (NARA)

THE CAMPAIGN

Having slugged their way through the Ardennes Forest and the Siegfried Line, Patton's Third US Army was fast approaching the Moselle River. As Patton's forces continued east, he expressed a little bit of envy over the success of his neighbors. To the south, Lieutenant-General Alexander "Sandy" Patch's Seventh US Army had reached the Rhine, though did not cross it, in late November 1944. To the north, Lieutenant-General William Simpson's Ninth US Army reached the Rhine on March 3, 1945, and four days later Lieutenant-General Courtney Hodges' First US Army had grabbed the bridge over the Rhine at Remagen. Nonetheless, Patton heartily congratulated his colleagues on their success even as he planned to do everything he could to upstage them. He was particularly keen on crossing the Rhine before British Field Marshal Bernard Montgomery and his 21st Army Group. On the same day that Hodges' 9th Armored Division captured the Ludendorff Bridge at Remagen, Patton's 4th Armored Division at last reached the river just north of Koblenz.

By March 9, Patton had already discussed with Lieutenant-General Omar Bradley the need to get his Third US Army heavily into the fight so as to forestall any efforts by Eisenhower and Montgomery to siphon off his divisions for the latter's offensive in the Ruhr plain. Thus, the 12th US Army Group commander discussed with both Patton and Patch, as well as Patch's superior at the 6th US Army Group, Lieutenant-General Jacob Devers, the need to launch an offensive in the Saar-Palatinate Triangle with the primary goal of getting the rest of the Army Group up to the Rhine River.

By March 10, the situation map showed a significant bulge westward in the German line, as the German leadership was intent on holding on to as much of the Siegfried Line as possible. It was an ideal setup for a pincer operation. Patton's Third US Army was deployed from just north of Saarbrücken up to Koblenz, following the northeast course of the Moselle River. To the south, Patch's Seventh US Army was deployed from just south of Saarbrücken and eastward toward Hagenau and the Rhine, and still facing the Siegfried Line. As early as mid-February, Eisenhower had already instructed Bradley and Devers to begin planning a joint operation to clear out the Saar-Palatinate Triangle. The essential idea was for the Third and Seventh US armies to coordinate the implosion of the German bulge in the region, but with Patton's forces playing second fiddle. However, Patton had no desire to wait on the Seventh US Army, which he deemed was moving too slowly. And of course, the last thing Patton wanted was to be in someone's shadow.

On March 10, Patton issued an Operational Directive outlining his plan to cross the Moselle River and advance southeast toward Bad Kreuznach. At this

The 3rd Battalion, 11th Infantry Regiment during the drive on the Moselle. It would be these men who would soon cross the Rhine at Nierstein. Until then, they have employed several captured German SdKfz 251 Ausf. D half-tracks to enhance their mobility, painting prominent white stars to avoid misidentification. In addition, nestled in the closest half-track is a commandeered civilian registered German motorcycle, probably a BMW R12. Both sides used motorcycles for messenger, liaison, and scouting purposes. (NARA)

time, the boundaries between the Third and Seventh Armies ran from Saarbourg along the Nahe River to Bad Kreuznach, and then on to Bingen on the Rhine River. Indeed, the original conception of the offensive as outlined by SHAEF and 12th US Army Group was to have Patch's Seventh US Army cross the Rhine somewhere between Mainz and Mannheim, while Patton's army engaged in diversionary efforts. Patton pressed Bradley for a modification to the plan, asking for a greater role in the campaign and assisting Patch's army to punch through the Siegfried Line by taking it in the flank. Bradley presented the idea to Eisenhower, who approved it in overall conception. However, even as late as March 13, Letter of Instruction No. 17 from Bradley's 12th US Army Group stipulated that Patton's army was only to advance up to the Rhine and then defend in place to allow Patch's army to cross the river.

Despite this "official" agenda, Patton had several months prior pegged out the Nierstein–Oppenheim site as a prospective crossing point, an area that lay precisely in the middle of the area planned for Patch's army. With this in mind, the unfolding of events would imply that Patton had already determined to press on beyond the army boundaries on the map and forge his Rhine crossing in Patch's zone of advance. Never shy about pushing the envelope, Patton was both an excellent planner and opportunist, and he was more than willing to create situations that he could exploit against both his enemies and his own superiors.

Patch's offensive, codenamed *Undertone*, was to begin March 15. Patton decided to launch his attack two days prior. Therefore, even as some of his units were still clearing up the western side of the Moselle, Patton's army transitioned from pursuit to a major offensive. It is of interest to note that unless created by a superior, there appears to be no indication that Patton ever provided codenames for his operations. Instead, he and his staff created multiple courses of actions that he dubbed as "Plan A," "Plan B," and so forth. They then chose the course of action that best corresponded to most effectively exploiting an enemy's weakness while accomplishing the mission.

Patton's plan was significantly different from Patch's. Whereas the latter intended to launch an attack across his entire front, Patton decided to focus on his left, or northern flank. To do this, he reduced Middleton's corps to one division and a cavalry group, the 87th Infantry and 6th respectively, and concentrated his army's combat power in Eddy's XII Corps. The XII Corps was to attack first only on its left flank, leaving its right flank operationally inactive. Moreover, Walker's XX Corps was to pause initially as well. This would allow XII Corps to plunge behind the German lines as far and as fast as the situation would allow. In this regard, the prospects looked good, despite the fact that the Germans had been trying to reinforce the Moselle River line.

As the Germans prepared to meet the next wave of Allied assaults in the West, Hitler decided that it was time to once more dispense with the venerable Generalfeldmarschall von Rundstedt. He had been relieved as commander of Oberbefehlshaber (OB) West on July 2, 1944, but was reinstated on September 3 so as to rectify the disastrous situation that had overtaken German arms in France. When he returned, von Rundstedt did so with numerous stipulations, including the ability to more freely move units about to restructure the forces on hand and to determine when and where to fight. This notion of freedom of action did not sit well with Hitler, and during the Ardennes Offensive he began to meddle increasingly with von Rundstedt's decisions. By February 1945, Hitler was determined to relieve him again, blaming him for the growing debacle in the West. The capture of the Remagen Bridge was the last straw.

Hitler called upon Generalfeldmarschall Albert Kesselring, who was in command of Heeresgruppe C in Italy. However, Kesselring was still recovering from a serious car accident, in which his command vehicle collided with an artillery piece on October 23, 1944. When meeting with Hitler on March 9, Kesselring demurred, but his objections were overruled. By March 10, Kesselring was at the OB West headquarters in the castle of Ziegenberg, and after being briefed by his chief of staff General Siegfried Westphal, Kesselring headed out to his subordinate headquarters. He discovered that the situation was much graver than presented to him by those close to Hitler. OB West commanded 55 weak divisions, most at 50 percent strength or less. He learned from Generalfeldmarschall Walter Model, the commander of Heeresgruppe B, that the means to destroy the American bridgehead at Remagen were not at hand. He also learned how serious the situation was for Heeresgruppe G, commanded by SS-Oberst-Gruppenführer Paul Hausser.

Accompanied by Hausser, Kesselring visited the headquarters of General Hans Felber's 7.Armee located near Kastellaun. They were briefed that Patton's Third US Army was about to launch an offensive, and there had been unmistakable signs of preparation along the lower Moselle just southwest of Koblenz. The critical problem was that Felber's army was short of everything. But while things looked desperate, it was still believed that the front could hold if sufficient reserves were available. The question was whether or not Patton would give them the time needed.

For 7.Armee, the unit that was to receive the brunt of Patton's attack was Bürcky's 159.Volksgrenadier-Division. This unit had just recently moved into the line after having absorbed thousands of new recruits and replacements and receiving but a few weeks to train, and Bürcky naturally protested what he saw was his division's premature commitment. However, the pressing need of the moment was more urgent, and 159.Volksgrenadier-Division became the centerpiece of LXXXIX.Armee-Korps under General Gustav Höhne, whose headquarters had been transferred north from the Hagenau sector of Alsace. The 159. was Höhne's best division, fielding around 9,000 men, though in desperate need of more training. He had been promised reinforcements in the form of 6.SS-Gebirgs-Division "Nord," but it was still in transit, and only the reconnaissance battalion had arrived on the right of Bürcky's division.

An infantryman's life was one of near constant hardship, taking the lion's share of casualties and enduring the misery of the weather and Spartan field conditions. In this case, a 4th Infantry Division soldier digs in during the advance to the Moselle River, March 6, 1945. The 4th Division would soon be transferred to Patch's Seventh US Army to support its soon to be launched Operation *Undertone*. (NARA)

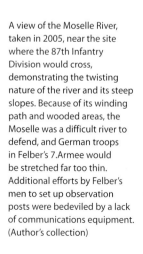

Troops of the 11th Infantry Regiment of Irwin's 5th Infantry Division prepare to cross the Moselle River, March 7, 1945. At this time, the weather was still cold and rainy, and the soldiers had to endure wet and muddy conditions during the advance, and many of those present in this photo are not wearing rubber overshoes. This often led to cases of immersion and trench foot, debilitating conditions that could quickly reduce a combat unit to non-effectiveness. (NARA)

Bürcky was under no illusions. Not only was his division not fully integrated, it also was thin on critical equipment. While he had both a towed antitank gun battalion and a self-propelled tank destroyer company, the actual numbers on hand were below authorization. Moreover, his artillery was weak, both in numbers and actual firepower. He had one battalion with 105mm howitzers, but the second battalion of 75mm howitzers authorized to a Volksgrenadier unit was a poor substitute for the heavier guns that used to equip German divisions. Because of shortages, heavier guns were typically grouped into Volks-Artillerie-Korps formations and controlled by more senior commanders.

Another factor facing Bürcky was the length of frontage he was required to defend. Hitler may have insisted that a Volksgrenadier division could defend 15km, but for Bürcky's soldiers this was scant comfort. While his frontage may have been a tolerable 20km as the crow flies, the winding nature of the Moselle River meant that the actual frontage was almost twice that. The river cuts a deep valley with steep slopes through the region, and the twists and turns and wooded terrain made lateral observation difficult. Moreover, defending a river properly was not a static operation. One of the more effective techniques was to maintain bridgeheads on the opposite bank so as to launch sharp counterattacks against an opponent to keep his troops off balance and disrupt his own assault plans. During the first week of March, 7.Armee had attempted to keep a number of bridgeheads on the northwest bank of the Moselle, but these were systematically reduced and eliminated by Patton's troops.

A view of the Moselle River, taken in 2005, near the site where the 87th Infantry Division would cross, demonstrating the twisting nature of the river and its steep slopes. Because of its winding path and wooded areas, the Moselle was a difficult river to defend, and German troops in Felber's 7.Armee would be stretched far too thin. Additional efforts by Felber's men to set up observation posts were bedeviled by a lack of communications equipment. (Author's collection)

For Bürcky, his problem was that he simply did not have the infantry to provide coverage for the front, a problem made only worse when he was ordered to detach his engineer battalion to assist 276.Volksgrenadier-Division to his right until 6.SS-Gebirgs-Division arrived. All he could do was establish strongpoints at likely crossing points and key avenues of approach, and otherwise set up observation posts to put eyes on blind spots where the river would bend. Even these were problematic, as he lacked sufficient communications equipment and signal personnel to make these effective, being deficient in radios, telephones, and field cables. Bürcky estimated that if he could have had just two more weeks, he could have had the division properly trained and many of the deficiencies would have been remedied. If there was one thing German generals had learned, it was that Patton was not the type of opponent to give one adequate preparatory time.

Help was on the way for Höhne's skeletal corps in the form of 6.SS-Gebirgs-Division "Nord." This unit had just finished enduring a significant ordeal near Trier, after the city's capture by Patton's troops. During their counterattack of March 7, the SS troops had gained about 5km against stiff resistance from the US 94th Infantry Division. Late in the afternoon, the engagement became a combined-arms infantry and tank battle, with American tankers from the 778th Tank Battalion exchanging volleys with *Sturmgeschutzen* and Hetzers. While the Americans lost a total of 10 tanks, the SS troops lost six *Sturmgeschutzen* and five antitank guns, along with over 750 killed, wounded, and missing, losses they could ill afford.

By the next day, 6.SS-Gebirgs-Division was pulled out of the line and placed in reserve, being prepared to meet the crisis building near Koblenz. A few days later, SS-Gebirgsjäger Regiment 11 "Reinhard Heydrich" was on the move, truck bound and heading north to its assembly area at Boppard on the Rhine. The reconnaissance battalion, being more mobile, preceded them, arriving on the right flank of 159.Volksgrenadier-Division on March 13, which was good news for Bürcky as he could now get his engineer battalion back. The first SS elements to arrive consisted of a heavy weapons company, supported by engineer, antitank, and 75mm gun platoons, all under the command of SS-Hauptsturmführer Karl-Hans Scheu. Routed through Boppard along the Rhine, Scheu's small battlegroup would quickly make its presence felt.

CROSSING THE MOSELLE

While most of Patton's forces either fought around Trier or mopped up the area west of the Moselle, Eddy's XII Corps quickly prepared to cross the Moselle and drive southeast. Irwin's 5th Infantry Division was to be on the right, with Earnest's 90th Infantry Division on the left, with their crossing points about 15–20km upstream from Koblenz. Once they established a firm bridgehead, the 4th Armored Division was to follow and exploit the breach. To his superiors, Patton's attack was to merely clean up the Saar-Palatinate Triangle and to assist Patch's Seventh US Army to advance through the Siegfried Line and then on to the Rhine. But Patton had other ideas.

One of the key aces up Patton's sleeve was his engineers. Equipped with pontoon, treadway, and Bailey bridges of varying capacity and supported by US Navy personnel operating various types of landing craft, many of

Initial Moselle crossing, March 13–14, 1945

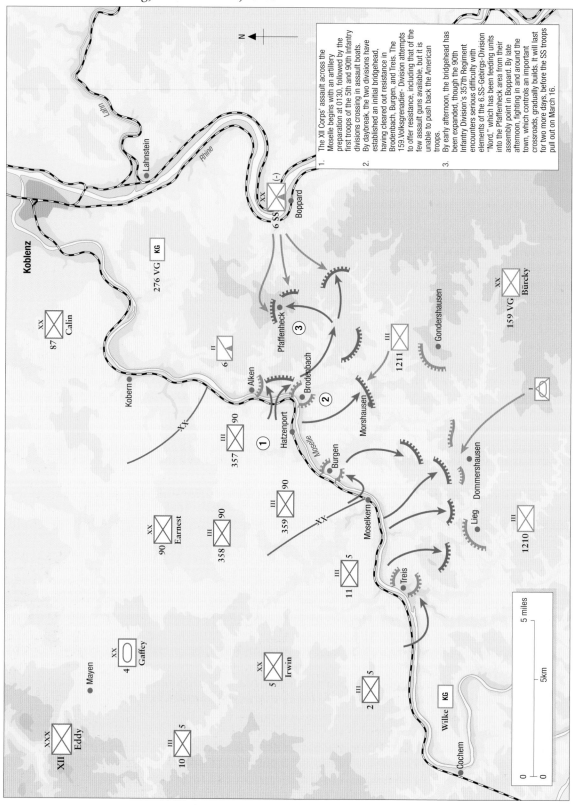

1. The XII Corps' assault across the Moselle begins with an artillery preparation at 0130, followed by the first troops of the 5th and 90th Infantry divisions crossing in assault boats. By daybreak, the two divisions have established an initial bridgehead, having cleared out resistance in Brodenbach, Burgen, and Treis. The 159.Volksgrenadier- Division attempts to offer resistance, including that of the few assault guns available, but it is unable to push back the American troops.

2. By early afternoon, the bridgehead has been expanded, though the 90th Infantry Division's 357th Regiment encounters serious difficulty with elements of the 6.SS-Gebirgs-Division "Nord," which has been feeding units into the Pfaffenheck area from their assembly point in Boppard. By late afternoon, fighting in and around the town, which controls an important crossroads, gradually builds. It will last for two more days, before the SS troops pull out on March 16.

these units were held in rear areas along major routes of advance to respond quickly once any river crossing became imminent or established. Once activated, they were prepared to advance rapidly to the point of decision to throw across a bridge. The most heavily organized stockpile of bridging equipment was held near Toul, France, just west of Nancy, and it was not until the XII Corps neared the Rhine that this equipment was moved in a circuitous route to an advanced dump located by Alzey, Germany.

The various bridges came in different configurations, being either fixed or floating, with most capable of handling any weight of vehicle within the army. The importance of the engineers in Patton's operations can be underscored by the number and length of bridges laid during March 1945. Having already forged across the Prüm and Kyll rivers, the operations to cross the Saar, Moselle, and Rhine would bring the monthly total to 341 bridges laid of all types, and totaling 44,073ft, or almost 13.5km. These efforts exceeded any previous monthly total set within the Third US Army. Besides bridging, engineer units also assisted in the initial crossing, often with small storm boats followed by motorized assault boats and pontoon rafts to move heavy equipment across. Pushing all of this equipment to the point of decision was a monumental task that required foresight, rapid but careful staff planning, route delegation, and effective small-unit leadership to overcome the never-ending glitches that threatened timely execution. Indeed, planning for the Rhine crossing alone began in August 1944. Having already crossed over 20 major rivers, Patton's staff and engineers had developed their methods to a serious art form.

But even with all of the planning, gaps appeared. As Patton's troops cleared the western bank of the Moselle, some of them failed to secure outpost towns along the river. This oversight was adroitly exploited by some of the German units, especially the enterprising SS-Hauptsturmführer Scheu. On arriving in his sector, he found himself opposite the village of Gondorf, which lay across the Moselle. In the early hours of March 13, Scheu led a reinforced patrol in small boats across the river, only to find that the village was unoccupied. In addition, another unit crossed over at Kobern just to the north. Having assisted village elders in removing German explosives from two railroad viaducts, Scheu was discouraged to find that these same people were all too eager to point out the positions of his men to an American motorized patrol of the 2nd Cavalry Group. It was obvious that the locals were not too keen to see any fighting that would see further devastation to their homes. By March 15, Scheu was compelled to fall back to the east of the Moselle, being too weak to seriously disrupt the river crossing efforts of XII Corps.

With the few German bridgeheads over the Moselle eliminated by March 13, Eddy's assault divisions were able to begin their crossing. Both the 5th and 90th Infantry divisions were deployed with two regiments forward and one in reserve. During the hours of darkness, storm boats and other assault craft were rushed to assembly points

Rubber boats were part of the equipment used to make initial assault river crossings. The first men across typically paddled their way on such rubber boats or on 10-man assault boats, using silence to create tactical surprise. Once the initial landing spots had been secured, the next waves followed in motorized boats such as Navy LCVPs. Here, a boat is being inflated with a compressor, a piece of equipment typically assigned to engineer units. (NARA)

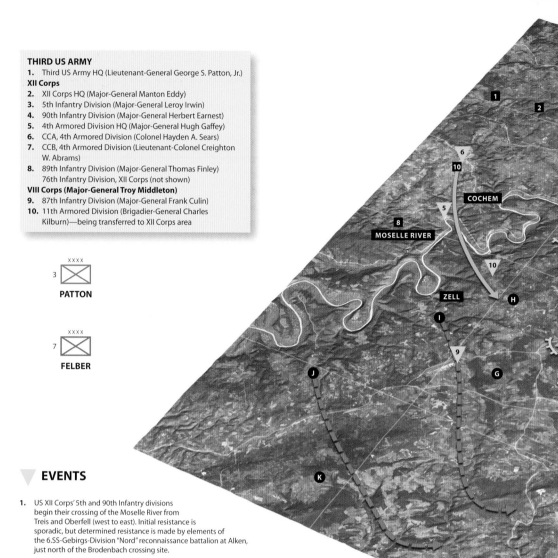

THIRD US ARMY
1. Third US Army HQ (Lieutenant-General George S. Patton, Jr.)

XII Corps
2. XII Corps HQ (Major-General Manton Eddy)
3. 5th Infantry Division (Major-General Leroy Irwin)
4. 90th Infantry Division (Major-General Herbert Earnest)
5. 4th Armored Division HQ (Major-General Hugh Gaffey)
6. CCA, 4th Armored Division (Colonel Hayden A. Sears)
7. CCB, 4th Armored Division (Lieutenant-Colonel Creighton W. Abrams)
8. 89th Infantry Division (Major-General Thomas Finley)
   76th Infantry Division, XII Corps (not shown)

VIII Corps (Major-General Troy Middleton)
9. 87th Infantry Division (Major-General Frank Culin)
10. 11th Armored Division (Brigadier-General Charles Kilburn)—being transferred to XII Corps area

▼ EVENTS

1. US XII Corps' 5th and 90th Infantry divisions begin their crossing of the Moselle River from Treis and Oberfell (west to east). Initial resistance is sporadic, but determined resistance is made by elements of the 6.SS-Gebirgs-Division "Nord" reconnaissance battalion at Alken, just north of the Brodenbach crossing site.

2. Bürcky's 159.Volksgrenadier-Division attempts an initial rally to hold strongpoints just east of the Moselle, destroying or damaging almost 30 tanks in the process in the area around Morshausen.

3. Brenner's 6.SS-Gebirgs-Division "Nord," minus its SS-Gebirgsjäger-Regiment 12, begins to arrive in strength in the Rhine–Moselle Triangle, engaging in a fierce firefight with 90th US Infantry Division troops on March 14 for the key crossroad of Pfaffenheck and surrounding villages.

4. Gaffey's 4th Armored Division crosses the Moselle on March 15, positioning Colonel Sears' CCA and Lieutenant-Colonel Abrams' CCB in the infantry bridgeheads in preparation to exploit.

5. Finley's 89th Infantry Division engages in limited holding attacks between Zell and Cochem along the Moselle River front of Oriola's XIII.Armee-Korps, March 14–15. Oriola has little information as to events to his north and is refused permission to withdraw from the river. Finley's division establishes a small bridgehead.

6. Kilburn's 11th Armored Division, just detached from Middleton's VIII Corps, assembles to the northwest of the 89th Division on March 15 in preparation to exploit any additional bridgeheads over the Moselle.

7. Culin's 87th Infantry Division crosses the Moselle into the Rhine–Moselle Triangle on March 15, and begins offensive operations to capture Koblenz. Kampfgruppe Koblenz, under Oberstleutnant Löffler, puts up only modest resistance, and the city falls two days later.

8. On March 16, the 4th Armored Division, supported by a motorized infantry regiment, continues exploitation operations, lunging south to the Nahe River in the vicinity of Bad Kreuznach after punching through the Soonwald. The 5th Infantry Division covers the growing western flank. German attempts to set up a blocking position on the Simmer River in the vicinity of Simmern are brushed aside.

9. Oriola receives orders to march 2.Panzer-Division and 246.Volksgrenadier-Division southeast and counterattack against the 4th Armored Division's advance. Kühn's 246.Volksgrenadier-Division must travel 30km in one day under

American air attack and crossing the significant terrain feature of the Idarwald. Lauchert's 2.Panzer-Division encounters roadblocks set up by German civilians to instead block the American advance, slowing their progress.

10. On March 17, Kilburn's 11th Armored Division passes through a recently established bridgehead by the 87th Division, and begins to advance rapidly southeast in the sector vacated by Oriola's troops. Kilburn receives orders to advance on Worms on the Rhine River.

11. Lauchert's 2.Panzer-Division is ordered to attack on its own, without 246. Volksgrenadier-Division, with but six tanks and assault guns and 200 infantry. Starting from the area east of Kirn, Lauchert's division advances 10km before the attack stalls. He is forced to withdraw, his division now expended. The 246. Volksgrenadier-Division, still marching from the southwest, is ordered to instead attach itself to Förtsch's 1.Armee.

12. With the success of the American advance, Brenner is ordered to withdraw his 6.SS-Gebirgs-Division "Nord," along with the remnants of the 276.Volksgrenadier-Division, across the Rhine at the ferry site at Boppard. This movement is completed by March 18, and the 90th Infantry Division takes Boppard soon after.

13. The 90th Infantry Division sweeps southward along the west bank of the Rhine, clearing it of pockets of enemy resistance and taking Bingen by March 19.

14. On March 17, the 4th Armored Division moves around Bad Kreuznach, but must stop for almost a day so that the city can be cleared of German resistance.

INITIAL ATTACK ON THE LOWER MOSELLE, MARCH 14–17, 1945

The exploitation of the US 4th Armored Division and other units behind 7.Armee up to Bad Kreuznach and the Nahe River.

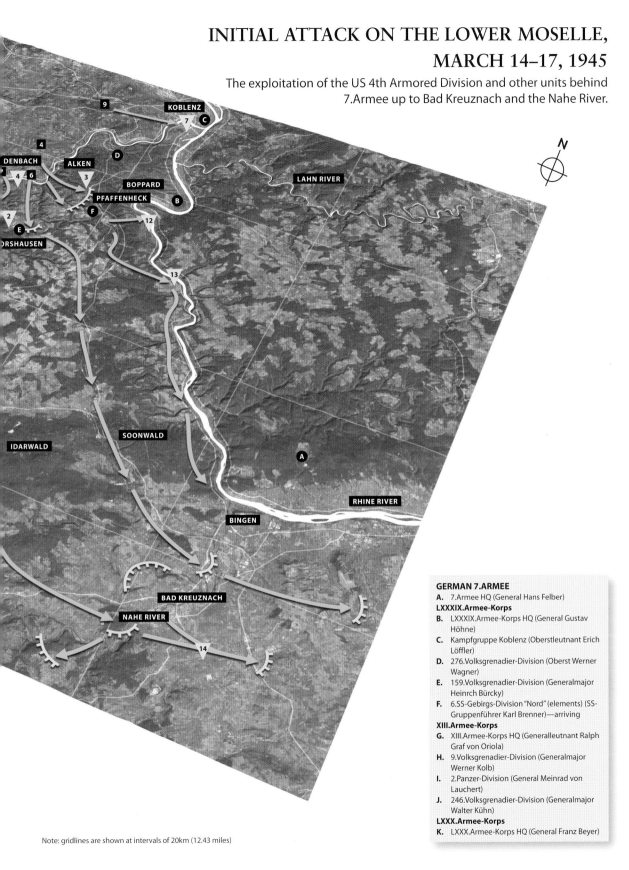

GERMAN 7.ARMEE
- **A.** 7.Armee HQ (General Hans Felber)

LXXXIX.Armee-Korps
- **B.** LXXXIX.Armee-Korps HQ (General Gustav Höhne)
- **C.** Kampfgruppe Koblenz (Oberstleutnant Erich Löffler)
- **D.** 276.Volksgrenadier-Division (Oberst Werner Wagner)
- **E.** 159.Volksgrenadier-Division (Generalmajor Heinrch Bürcky)
- **F.** 6.SS-Gebirgs-Division "Nord" (elements) (SS-Gruppenführer Karl Brenner)—arriving

XIII.Armee-Korps
- **G.** XIII.Armee-Korps HQ (Generalleutnant Ralph Graf von Oriola)
- **H.** 9.Volksgrenadier-Division (Generalmajor Werner Kolb)
- **I.** 2.Panzer-Division (General Meinrad von Lauchert)
- **J.** 246.Volksgrenadier-Division (Generalmajor Walter Kühn)

LXXX.Armee-Korps
- **K.** LXXX.Armee-Korps HQ (General Franz Beyer)

Note: gridlines are shown at intervals of 20km (12.43 miles)

near the riverbank, and by 0130hrs on March 14, a two-hour preparatory bombardment heralded the start of the crossing. A half hour later, the first assault troops entered the water, with only one battalion of the 11th Infantry Regiment of the 5th Division delayed for almost two hours when their boats were late in arriving. As dawn approached, the Moselle River was shrouded in mist, both natural and artificial, the later from the smoke generator units that had been deployed to conceal the crossing. For Irwin's boys, the leap across the Moselle was already a huge success, with the assault regiments probing into Treis and ascending the slopes of the eastern bank to seize the high ground beyond. By the close of the day, houses along the river had been cleared and the 1135th Engineer Group had built a Class 40 treadway bridge across the river at Hatzenport. Enemy losses from 159.Volksgrenadier-Division had so far been about 160 in killed, wounded, and captured.

The assault of the 90th Infantry Division seemed to go just as well at first. Troops of the 357th Infantry Regiment pushed across the river just north of Brodenbach, and by daylight had run into 200 enemy of Grenadier-Regiment 1211 ensconced in the town. Despite being outflanked to their west by the 359th Infantry Regiment, this enemy combat group put up a stout resistance until about noon, when they quickly withdrew up a draw in the direction of the castle of Ehrenberg. Concurrently, elements of the 3rd Battalion of the 357th Infantry Regiment probed north into Alken, only to find the rapidly growing presence of 6.SS-Gebirgs-Division. In the 359th sector, one battalion advanced along the river toward Burgen, where it ran into another enemy strongpoint of about 200 men. Burgen was cleared by 0830hrs, and by early afternoon the assault battalions of the 90th Division had pushed inland around 4km.

For Bürcky and his troops, the artillery bombardment had been anything but random, the Americans having registered their guns well and knocking out his fragile communications network. As the crossing developed, the commander of Grenadier-Regiment 1211 had attempted to inform the division headquarters as early as 0500hrs, but Bürcky did not get any details until 0800hrs. The loss of three precious hours would prove to be decisive in his division's early collapse. Nevertheless, Bürcky reacted quickly and went road-bound in his command car to gain more knowledge as to what was precisely happening. In the meantime, his staff managed to make contact with Höhne's headquarters, and LXXXIX.Armee-Korps dispatched an infantry battalion and eight assault guns for support. They also got their own reserve on the move, a single infantry company that had to march close to 20km on foot to reach the area of action.

Two of the dispatched assault guns managed to link up with infantry of Grenadier-Regiment 1211 in Morshausen, the same unit that had just fled Brodenbach. Their arrival was none too soon, as infantry from the 359th began to advance into the edge of the town from the nearby woods. A running battle enveloped the village streets, with the sound of rifle and machine-gun fire sporadically interlaced with the sharp crack of the German assault guns and the swoosh of American bazookas. Lacking any armor support, the Americans desperately fired off all of their bazooka rounds in a vain attempt to knock out the assault guns. Word of their plight reached regimental headquarters, who doubled their efforts to float several tanks and tank destroyers across the river to lend a hand. When this heavy support at last arrived, the Germans pulled out.

Despite some initial resistance, Earnest's men had established their own firm bridgehead, with a heavy pontoon bridge built at Moselkern just before noon. Earlier, a footbridge that was being laid in the 5th Infantry Division's sector had broken loose, with the pontoons and sections floating downstream to collide with a 90th Infantry Division bridge under construction, delaying its completion by several hours. Nevertheless, by the end of the first day, Eddy's XII Corps was firmly in control on the opposite bank of the Moselle, with three bridges built that could carry heavy vehicle traffic. Both divisions expanded their foothold, with the 5th Infantry Division reaching Lütz and clearing Treis along the river, while the 90th Infantry Division cleared Herschwiesen and reached the edge of Pfaffenheck before resistance started to stiffen considerably. That night, the 4th Armored Division, lying in wait north of the crossings, was alerted to begin moving the next day. By 1200hrs on March 15, Combat Command A began crossing the bridges over the Moselle.

TO THE NAHE RIVER

The situation was critical, not only for 159.Volksgrenadier-Division, but for the entire 7.Armee. Felber and his staff now stared at the very crisis they had predicted only days before, and desperate calls to Heeresgruppe G resulted in several infantry units being dispatched to the area. However, at this moment three of the most effective German units were either scattered or completely in the wrong place. 6.SS-Gebirgs-Division "Nord" was already split apart across the entire army front. But 17.SS-Panzergrenadier-Division "Götz von Berlichingen" was currently fighting before the bunkers of the Siegfried Line south near Zweibrücken, while schwere Panzerjäger-Abteilung 653, with its powerful Jagdtigers,was north of Hagenau in Alsace. While the Jagdtiger was a clumsy beast, its 128mm cannon could dominate anything within range. Thus, at the moment of crisis, Heeresgruppe G and 7.Armee had failed to deploy effectively at the critical point of decision.

By the afternoon of March 14, Bürcky had determined to set a new main line of resistance from Gondershausen to Lieg in an effort to contain the growing American bridgehead, while his artillery engaged identified American units that were advancing. But by 1700hrs, the Americans pushed through Lieg and shattered the nascent line of 159.Volksgrenadier-Division. Most of Bürcky's division was now being inexorably pressed to the south and southeast, away from contact with not only the rest of Höhne's LXXXIX. Armee-Korps but their own Grenadier-Regiment 1211. Moreover, the artillery had to displace and thus the support fires began to drop off. Torn asunder and overrun, Bürcky's division crumbled and the Third US Army's prisoner count swelled to over 6,000 by March 14. As a Volksgrenadier division was not designed for mobile combat, to be placed in such a situation only increased the odds against it. However, all was not lost, as the more experienced officers and NCOs knew they could infiltrate their way to a new line of resistance if given a chance, and if the enemy units had not consolidated their positions.

On March 15, Gaffey's 4th Armored Division began to rapidly cross the Moselle, with one combat command in each of the bridgeheads established by the two infantry divisions. Once past the steep slopes of the Moselle, the terrain becomes gently rolling hills punctuated by woodlands separated by significant gaps, allowing for rapid movement between the woods. Elements of 159.Volksgrenadier-Division continued to offer some resistance in the area of the 5th Infantry Division, and through the day Bürcky's antitank and assault guns managed to knock out or damage about 30 American tanks. Nevertheless, Bürcky had already received orders to withdraw what he could to the Nahe River near Simmern unter Dhaun with the intent of denying the Americans any crossing point there. Early on, the Nahe had been established as the next defensive line to hold, and tactical leaders in the German units knew this line to be their rally point. Their movement south choked the roads, a mass of vehicles of all description intermingled with horse- and hand-drawn carts along with disparate artillery pieces towed by equally disparate means of transport. Traffic control virtually collapsed as refugees joined the columns, and German commanders attempting to rally their troops became entangled in the chaos.

As these columns fled south and east, they became the target of the XIX Tactical Air Command (TAC), whose P-47s and P-51s, guided by loitering observation planes like the L-4 Grasshopper and L-5 Sentinel, swooped down upon them like a hungry pack of wolves. Just prior to the crossing of the Moselle, the weather had been poor, but by March 14 the skies had cleared. While armored vehicles were a difficult target for the flyboys, the soft-skinned trucks and wagons were meat on the table. Brigadier-General Otto Weyland's pilots utilized a combination of machine guns and general purpose bombs and rockets to blast the columns. Eddy's XII Corps was primarily supported by the 362nd Fighter Group, which flew 25 missions and claimed 229 trucks, 15 armored vehicles, and 207 railroad cars and locomotives. On March 15, Weyland's pilots, enabled by the excellent weather, flew a record 643 sorties, not only hitting fleeing German troops and destroying over 250 vehicles of all types and over 400 railroad cars and locomotives, but striking depots and marshaling yards in rear areas such as Friedberg and Wiesbaden.

Even as the 159.Volksgrenadier-Division attempted to displace southward toward the Nahe River, all was not roses for Eddy's men. The 90th Infantry Division, particularly the 357th Regiment under Lieutenant-Colonel John Mason, discovered to their discomfort increasing resistance on the northern flank from 6.SS-Gebirgs-Division. On March 14, they had already had to deal with one SS company in Alken commanded by SS-Hauptsturmführer Günther Degen. The Americans surrounded the unit, but after nearly being wiped out, they managed to break out and rejoin the rest of the division.

While still missing its SS-Gebirgsjäger Regiment 12 and some of its artillery, the rest of the SS division was being fed into the Rhine–Moselle Triangle by the hour and a growing battle was forming around the village of Pfaffenheck. The town was ensconced in a triangle of woods and controlled an important crossroad, with a black-top road leading north to Koblenz and the other east to Boppard on the Rhine. SS-Gruppenführer Karl Brenner was pulling his mountain troops through Boppard as fast as they could

While the weather in early March was not conducive to air operations, by the second week the conditions improved, allowing Weyland's XIX TAC to ravage German columns retreating to the east. Other columns were spotted by American observation aircraft, and then subjected to a hail of artillery fire from heavy guns. Advancing American troops witnessed a carnage only seen during the breakout from Normandy, the roads littered with smashed wagons and the broken bodies of men and beasts. This column was caught along the west bank of the Rhine River near Andernach. (US Army Signal Corps/The General George Patton Museum)

be transported and then pushing them westward along the winding road up a draw into Pfaffenheck. By the morning of March 15, SS-Gebirgsjäger Regiment 11 under SS-Standartenführer Helmut Raithel, supported by two light artillery batteries and a battery of assault guns and antitank guns, was deployed and launching small counterattacks at both Pfaffenheck and Udenhausen so as to blunt the American advance.

The American infantry in the area, mainly the 357th's 3rd Battalion, were supported by tanks of C Company of the 712th Tank Battalion. As the Americans occupied Pfaffenheck, Udenhausen, and Bucholz, they assumed that the Germans were retreating to the Rhine and thus settled down for a quiet night on March 14. The following day, things began to heat up some, but it was not until the 16th that the Germans launched their most serious counterattack. Brenner divided his force of over 3,000 men into two *Kampfgruppen*, one under Raithel and the other under the artillery commander, SS-Oberführer Johann Göbel. Raithel's consisted of two battalions supported by assault guns, with a sector of attack between Pfaffenheck and Udenhausen. Göbel's *Kampfgruppe* had one battalion supported by the engineers, antiaircraft, and artillery, and a tank destroyer platoon, and was to attack between Udenhausen and Bucholz. Heavy woods between Pfaffenheck and Bucholz precluded their ability to coordinate their attack.

In the predawn light, Raithel's group hit Pfaffenheck and drove the American infantry from the town. The Americans organized a dawn counterattack supported by five tanks and got into a furious firefight with the SS troops in an orchard near the village. Assault gun and antitank fire knocked out five Shermans, while the Germans poured fire from antiaircraft vehicles at the American infantry. During the fight, Pfaffenheck changed hands several times. By mid-afternoon, the two sides became entangled in the woods and the battle became hand-to-hand with the bodies of both Americans and Germans found in the same fighting positions. Despite the use of artillery and mortar fire, it came down to the doughboy with his M-1 rifle that stopped the German assaults. As the official history of the 357th Infantry Regiment put it, "the Germans were using with extravagance their only remaining source of defense—the bodies of their soldiers." As night came on, more American tanks showed up and the Germans withdrew, having received orders to cross the Rhine to the east bank after setting up roadblocks to delay the American pursuit. Among the dead left behind was SS-Hauptsturmführer Degen, who had been mortally wounded near Pfaffenheck.

Even as one regiment of the 90th Infantry Division slugged it out with SS troops on the left flank, the 4th Armored Division crossed the Moselle on March 15, and positioned itself to breakout from the bridgehead. Combat Command A, under Colonel Hayden A. Sears, crossed the river in the southern part of the 90th Infantry Division's bridgehead, while Combat Command B, led by Lieutenant-Colonel Creighton W. Abrams crossed further upriver in the 5th Infantry Division's sector. Part of the planned exploitation was to motorize

While the infantry endured much of the misery of the field, the life of a tanker was one of constant hard work. Whether it was maintenance on tracks, pulling damaged engines or, as in this case of 11th Armored Division tankers, loading up ammunition, a tanker could be expected to do many heavy tasks, most of them by hand. Moreover, such tasks seemed never-ending. (US Army Signal Corps/The General George Patton Museum)

an infantry regiment, with the 90th's 359th Regiment attached to Gaffey's combat commands. This method of exploitation demonstrated a marked difference between how Patton's forces managed such situations compared to the other American armies. Patton's Third US Army typically would motorize an infantry regiment and attach it to an armored division to gain the maximum amount of speed, while other American army commanders tended to attach an armored combat command to a foot-speed infantry division to provide it with more firepower. The way Patton handled armored formations demonstrated a completely different mindset about warfare, and was one of the reasons why the Germans feared him most.

With a motorized regiment in tow, CCA and CCB swept southeast toward Bad Kreuznach and the Nahe River. To do so, they had to cross the Hunsrück, the Simmer River, and the Soonwald. It was at the Soonwald, just before the Nahe River, where Gaffey's tankers could encounter significant difficulties if German forces had time to settle into defensive positions. Sears and Abrams had no intention of letting this happen. Shadowed by the aerial umbrella of Weyland's XIX TAC, the tanks and half-track-borne infantry led the way, followed by the motorized infantry that fanned out to the flanks to mop up stray German units. American commanders likened the developing situation to another Falaise Pocket. German commanders on the spot likened it to another Stalingrad, with two armies on the block.

Bürcky's division now disintegrated in the debacle, though enterprising small-unit leaders managed to slip broken remnants toward the Nahe River. Concurrently, rear echelon elements got caught up in the rout, with some being overrun while others were strafed by American fighter-bombers. Making matters more dramatic, American artillery observation planes circled overhead, directing the guns from division to corps level onto lucrative targets. On March 15, at the village of Karbach just west of St Goar on the Rhine, a German artillery unit being towed to a Rhine crossing site was spotted and targeted by 8in. howitzers. The heavy shells blasted the carts and limbers, tossing the mangled bodies of horses onto the shattered roofs of the village, a scene of carnage that astonished even the hardened troops of the 90th Infantry. Höhne's LXXXIX.Armee-Korps retreated to the east with plans to cross the Rhine south of Koblenz. Besides the lion's share of the 6.SS-Gebirgs-Division, Bürcky's Grenadier-Regiment 1211 was forced to fall back to the east as well, losing all contact with the division headquarters.

March 15 also saw the start of Patch's Seventh US Army's planned offensive in northern Alsace, codenamed *Undertone*. With nine infantry divisions abreast from Saarbrücken to the Wissembourg Gap, and supported by the 6th, 14th, and later the 13th Armored divisions, Patch's men took on 1.Armee under General Hermann Förtsch and pushed north toward the border with Germany. The 103rd Infantry Division tangled briefly with the Jagdtigers of schwere Panzerjäger-Abteilung 653 before this unit was withdrawn northward in a belated effort to stem the collapse of 7.Armee. Concurrently, Patton's XX Corps under Major-General Walker began its attack against the flank of the Siegfried Line along the Franco-German border east of Luxembourg.

Malcolm Fletcher was a Private First Class machine gunner in the 2nd Battalion, 101st Infantry Regiment of the 26th Infantry Division, who was engaged in clearing out pillboxes as part of the XX Corps' attack. Advancing eastward from Saarbourg, Fletcher and his fellow soldiers, supported by P-47s, flanked the pillboxes one by one and eventually cleared them out. On

March 17, Fletcher's unit was motorized, becoming part of a combined-arms task force that began to move rapidly to the east. Resistance was scattered, though sometimes briefly intense, but in each case the Yankee Division's men went around the enemy and continued motoring east. By March 18, they were following the wake of the unleashed 10th Armored Division, which had moved out from the area near Trier to exploit the breakthrough. In this fashion, Walker's XX Corps began to collapse both the left flank of 7.Armee and the right flank of 1.Armee, smashing its way through the latter's LXXXII.Armee-Korps under General Walther Hahm and thus pushing their way out of the heavy Schwarzwälder Hochwald terrain.

For Felber and his headquarters staff, the rout developing on the 16th almost ended in disaster for them twice. As it was necessary to move the headquarters, the command group had to go road-bound during daylight. In the afternoon, having spotted American aircraft searching for targets, Felber's small command group dashed into a woods to hide. Almost as soon as they had done so, a column of 4th Armored Division tanks roared by, oblivious to the prize within reach. After this close call, Felber's staff pushed onward to the new headquarters site, and once more had to bolt into the woods to avoid another American column.

Even as the Seventh US Army, aided by Walker's corps, began to push the Germans out of Alsace, Gaffey's 4th Armored Division continued its spectacular lightning advance. By late March 15, the lead tanks of the division had passed through Simmern on the Simmer River and were moving around the eastern flank of Bürcky's reorganizing remnants of his division. On the following day, the advance slowed as Gaffey's tanks and mechanized infantry made contact with fragments of the 6.SS-Gebirgs-Division, which attempted to man roadblocks in the Soonwald. The delay was only momentary, and by the end of the day, the lead elements of the 4th Armored Division had reached the outskirts of Bad Kreuznach and established a bridgehead over the Nahe River south of the city at Bad Munster. Having already received verbal orders from Patton's headquarters to push on to Mainz and beyond, this advance now precipitated a minor crisis in command and control, for Patton's tankers were beginning to infringe on the Seventh US Army's boundary.

On March 17, Eisenhower and Patton met up with generals Patch and Devers at Patch's headquarters in Luneville, France to discuss a change in boundary. Patch was graciously accommodating, remarking that "we are all in the same army" and that the task was to beat the Germans. The boundary was subsequently shifted south, with the line running to Worms, and was finalized when Patch's army issued the Operations Instruction memo No. 99 of March 20. This gave Patton a free hand in the area between Mainz and Mannheim, an area he had already considered for a Rhine crossing months prior. Even as this decision was being made, the dormant center of Felber's army was at last beginning to stir.

Combat engineers were a critical component of high-tempo mobile combat, and bulldozers were an essential part of not only clearing the path of advance but improving roads in the rear areas to facilitate the movement of supplies and reinforcements. In this instance, a Caterpillar D7 Armored Bulldozer is being towed by a turretless M10 hull, designated M35, as a prime mover. This unit was supporting the 4th Armored Division during the drive to the Moselle. (NARA)

THE GERMAN RESPONSE

As the world seemed to come apart on both the right and left flanks, Generalluetnant Oriola's XIII.Armee-Korps had remained in what amounted to some form of fantasyland. Oriola's three divisions were probably the weakest in Felber's army and were positioned in the middle of the army's sector on the Moselle. Yet, during the first days of the Third US Army's offensive, his units had been only subjected to minor probes and efforts by the Americans to clear out any stragglers on the west side of the Moselle, culminating with the establishment of a small bridgehead by the 89th Infantry Division south of Cochem. With poor communications, Oriola and his staff had to rely upon the civilian telephone network to get any significant information. This was not unusual for German forces in the last months of the war, but what was truly peculiar was how Oriola's senior signal officer had to apply with telephone officials to receive permits to use the phone lines. Even more bizarre was the fact that Oriola, in a postwar interview, did not in any way see this as an obstacle, but considered it normal practice. While it is understandable that the telephone circuits could only handle a limited amount of traffic, why the military did not have immediate priority is nothing short of bewildering. It is even more bewildering that a senior army leader could not discern this.

Thus, even as 7.Armee crumbled, German commanders were still squabbling with local telephone bureaucrats to gain desperately needed access to telephone lines. Even more astonishing, the German commanders found that as their units were overrun, the Americans failed to block the phone network, thus allowing senior leaders to communicate with scattered units far behind enemy positions so as to coordinate their infiltration back to the main German line beyond the Rhine. Indeed, war can create some of the most peculiar circumstances that defy logic.

As the first days of Patton's offensive passed, XIII.Armee-Korps' headquarters could only obtain a sketchy picture as to what was happening. Oriola was aware that Höhne's corps to his right was being driven back, but he had no real idea how bad it was. But by March 16, his 9.Volksgrenadier-Division had pulled back its right flank to fill in for the 159.Volksgrenadier-Division that seemed to evaporate into thin air. Moreover, Oriola now received one of the most incredible orders imaginable. He was to pull his 2.Panzer-Division and 246.Volksgrenadier-Division off the Moselle and march southeast over 30km to attack the flank of the American penetration near Bad Kreuznach. And he was to attack on the morning of March 17.

Lauchert's 2.Panzer-Division was severely drained. He started his defense along the Moselle with fewer than two dozen tanks and assault guns, but by March 16 he was down to seven such vehicles, 200 infantry, and two artillery battalions. Because his division was so badly depleted, Lauchert's infantry was completely mobile on half-tracks and trucks, as were his artillery batteries. Thus, to make the movement to the assigned assembly near Simmern

Photographs of German troops in action in the last months of the war are rare. This picture, while taken of a counterattack in Pomerania on the Eastern Front, would highlight conditions for Lauchert's drained 2.Panzer-Division as they attempted a counterattack against the US XII Corps' advance down the west bank of the Rhine River. In just a few hours, the remnant of Lauchert's once proud division had virtually ceased to exist. (Heinrich Hoffmann/ullstein bild via Getty Images)

just northeast of Kirn was doable for him. However, for Generalmajor Walter Kühn's 246.Volksgrenadier-Division it was a different matter. Severely short of transport, his infantry would have to march with light packs and ammunition in daylight on roads swept by Patton's rampaging fighter-bombers. Moreover, they would have to traverse the Idarwald, a wooded spine that ran southwest to northeast and with a vertical drop of anywhere between 250 and 300m. The only consolation was that the Idarwald would help cover their movement, and by the time they emerged on the southeast edge it would be growing dark. But then came the prospect that Kühn would have to throw his mixed bag of troops into battle the next morning. While an infantry division could be expected to march 30km, this was only in the best of conditions and with properly trained men. Instead, the Landsers of 246. Volksgrenadier-Division were going to have to engage in what amounted to a forced foot march under the constant threat of air attack, and with personnel of varied conditioning and stamina. It was nothing short of madness.

Roadblocks erected by local German defense groups proved to be a nuisance to both friend and foe. Lauchert's 2.Panzer-Division was delayed when making its counterattack west of Bad Kreuznach, and American troops found them to occasionally be covered by sniper fire. Here, elements of the 76th Infantry Division's engineers dismantle a roadblock on what is today the Stromberger Strasse in Bingen, with the Rhine in the background. The castle-looking structure is today a winery. (NARA)

The attack was to involve the coordination of both divisions, while another attack was to be launched from the east toward Bad Kreuznach. But the need to attack at once was desperate, and Lauchert was ordered to go it alone and not wait for Kühn's division. His miniscule *Kampfgruppe* reached its assembly area but not without unexpected difficulties. Orders directly from Hitler to increase resistance had recently reached the villages and many had set up roadblocks. Rather than slowing the American advance, Lauchert's men had to dismantle these or go around them, thus losing two precious hours. At last they were positioned to attack by 0700hrs on the morning of the 17th. To Lauchert's advantage, the American flank was quite porous, and he also had tactical surprise. His tanks and panzergrenadiers advanced northeast up a bowling alley with the Soonwald to the north and another stretch of woodland to the south, slicing quickly through a screen of troops from the motorized 359th Infantry Regiment of the 90th Infantry Division and Task Force Breckenridge from the 5th Infantry Division. His spearhead managed to penetrate about 10km, reaching the villages of Winterbach and Rohbach before being ground to a halt and then forced back to his starting point. Lauchert now had but one tank and one assault gun and his exhausted remnants of infantry; 2.Panzer-Division had essentially ceased to exist.

As for the 246.Volksgrenadier-Division, Kühn's men at last reached Kirn mid-morning on the 17th, far too late to participate in the attack. Instead, the division was hastily handed off to Förtsch's 1.Armee, since communications with Oriola's corps were essentially lost. Thus, Oriola's corps now, too, began to disintegrate. Moreover, 1.Armee was beginning to be overrun from the west, as the 10th and 12th Armored divisions, the latter under Major-General Roderick Allen, accelerated their tempo in a drive to the east. The potential disaster unfolding had been explained to Kesselring by every senior leader in Heeresgruppe G. Instead, they were ordered to hold, and now raw truth was before them.

The destruction of SS-Gebirgsjäger-Regiment 12

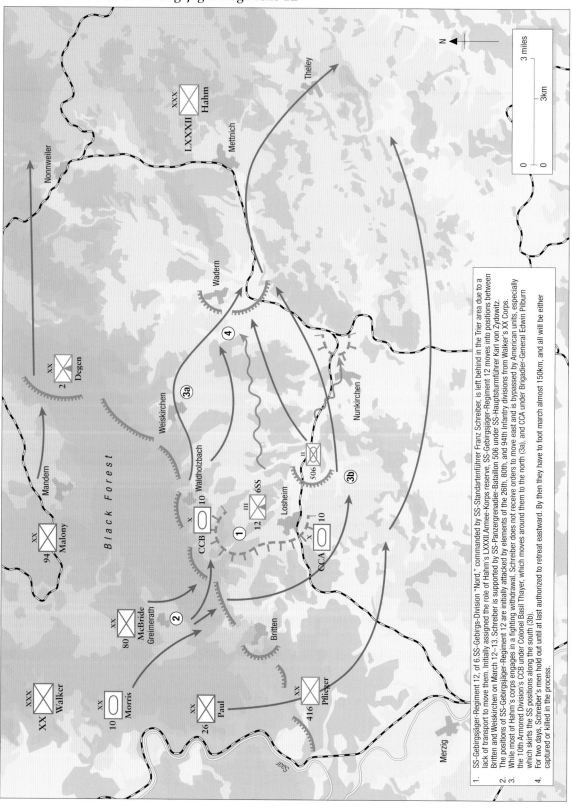

1. SS-Gebirgsjäger-Regiment 12, of 6.SS-Gebirgs-Division "Nord," commanded by SS-Standartenführer Franz Schreiber, is left behind in the Trier area due to a lack of transport to move them. Initially assigned the role of Hahm's LXXXII Armee-Korps reserve, SS-Gebirgsjäger-Regiment 12 moves into positions between Britten and Weiskirchen on March 12–13. Schreiber is supported by SS-Hauptsturmführer Karl von Zydowitz.
2. The positions of SS-Gebirgsjäger-Regiment 12 are initially attacked by elements of the 26th, 80th, and 94th Infantry divisions from Walker's XX Corps.
3. While most of Hahm's corps engages in a fighting withdrawal, Schreiber does not receive orders to move east and is bypassed by American units, especially the 10th Armored Division's CCB under Colonel Basil Thayer, which moves around them to the north (3a), and CCA under Brigadier-General Edwin Pilburn which skirts the SS positions along the south (3b).
4. For two days, Schreiber's men hold out until at last authorized to retreat eastward. By then they have to foot march almost 150km, and all will be either captured or killed in the process.

The growing disaster can best be illustrated by the fate of SS-Gebirgsjäger Regiment 12 from 6.SS-Gebirgs-Division "Nord." This regiment, under the command of SS-Standartenführer Franz Schreiber, had been forced to stay behind southeast of Trier partly due to lack of transport to move them north to the Koblenz area. The regiment initially assembled near Weiskirchen on March 12 and 13, serving as the reserve for Hahm's LXXXII.Armee-Korps of 1.Armee. When Walker's offensive began, Schreiber's regiment took up defensive positions between Britten and Waldhölzbach, and were supported at Losheim by 6.SS-Gebirgs-Division's reserve in the form of the SS-Panzergrenadier-Bataillon 506 under SS-Hauptsturmführer Karl von Zydowitz. On March 14, they were attacked by elements of the 26th, 80th, and 94th Infantry divisions. The SS troops grudgingly gave ground, falling back slowly toward the woods north of Losheim, even as American troops went around them.

By dark on March 16, Schreiber's men were essentially surrounded and cut off, having been bypassed by the 10th Armored Division's CCB to the north, under Colonel Basil G. Thayer and its CCA to the south, under Brigadier-General Edwin W. Pilburn. Schreiber also lost contact with SS-Panzergrenadier-Bataillon 506, which had been forced out of Losheim with heavy losses and fell back to the southeast, its commander now missing in action. Yet, this battalion managed to join in the withdrawal, surviving to fight another day east of the Rhine. As for Schreiber, he did not receive orders to withdraw until well into the night. Instructions were quickly passed about and the men fell in, road-marching in the dark toward Wadern on routes used just a few hours prior by the 10th Armored Division on their drive toward Sankt Wendel.

For almost two days they remained around Wadern, unaware that Hahm's divisions were engaged in a fighting withdrawal to the Rhine. By the time he received any information to this effect, the bulk of LXXXII.Armee-Korps was regrouping just west of the Germersheim bridgehead. To escape to the east, Schreiber's men would have to travel 150km through rapidly moving American units. He broke his remaining troops into small groups with orders to infiltrate back to the east. These *Ruckkampfern* began to move on March 19, but none made it back, with all being killed or captured. As for Schreiber, he managed to reach Westhofen near the Rhine with a few members of his staff before being captured on March 27. SS-Gebirgsjäger Regiment 12 "Michael Gaissmair," like many German units in the area, had simply vanished.

By March 18, Patton's entire army was on the move. On the northern edge, Middleton's VIII Corps, with the 87th Infantry Division, had already crossed the Moselle on March 15, and was pushing into Koblenz. Höhne had been ordered to withdraw his corps east of the Rhine, but was compelled to leave Kampfgruppe Koblenz in place with 1,800 men. This ad hoc unit was under the command of a highly decorated regimental-level officer, Oberstleutnant Erich Löffler. His bravery was already legendary when he took command at Koblenz, having earned a Knights Cross in Russia and four tank destruction badges for his right sleeve. The city was fairly well fortified from its days as an important strategic point, and was dominated by the huge medieval-era fortress of Ehrenbreitstein on the east side of the Rhine. Yet, despite this and Löffler's reputation, the defense of Koblenz was a desultory affair and lasted only two days. By March 19, the city was largely in American hands, with troops from the 345th Infantry Regiment refreshing themselves with champagne they had purchased locally with bundles of Reichsmarks they had found scattered in the streets. Löffler managed to escape across the Rhine with about 50 of his men, while almost 1,000 were taken prisoner. Many others had simply melted away.

To the south, east of Bad Kreuznach, the 4th Armored Division would encounter some stiffening resistance. Lieutenant-Colonel Albin "Al" Irzyk, the youthful commander of the 8th Tank Battalion and the lead element of CCA, had just radioed in that he had cleared the town of Sprendlingen, east of the city, when he was ordered to halt. The division's CCB had been ordered back to help clear out Bad Kreuznach, and Irzyk was held up to wait on them. Aggressive and decisive, Irzyk did not like being delayed for long, as he knew it would give the Germans time to set up some form of defense. Yet, the hours slipped by as he and his men waited impatiently for the order to push east through Sankt Johann and beyond. Irzyk used the time to adjust his position and seize some high ground nearby, but it was over seven hours before he was told he could press on. The results were predictable, as his lead platoon came under devastating 88mm fire from Sankt Johann. In seconds, five Shermans were on fire, their survivors filtering back to the west.

Calling in artillery, Irzyk made a rapid decision to charge the position himself, every gun on his tank blazing. Rolling downslope on the road, Irzyk's driver kept the accelerator floored as he took additional but inaccurate fire. Pushing into Sankt Johann, he passed one of his tanks, its commander too nervous to follow, crashed through a roadblock of piled logs, and pressed on towards Wolfsheim. The road seemed clear in the now growing darkness until he saw a flash and heard screams within his tank. They had just been hit by a panzerfaust, probably from a solitary German infantryman known as an *Einzelkämpfer*, or lone fighter. Irzyk and two of his crew were injured, and all five of them were now outside of their disabled tank hunkered down in a ditch. Expecting reinforcements to follow him, Irzyk saw to his horror that a half-track full of German infantry was rolling down the same road he had just cleared. Jumping back up on his tank, he manned a .30-caliber machine gun and poured fire into the open top of the vehicle. With bodies slumping, the German driver veered off the road and disappeared into a nearby wood. Moments later, the rest of Irzyk's battalion came rolling down the road to their rescue, and the attack could continue.

Despite delays experienced by such units as Irzyk's tank battalion, the XII and XX Corps were now motoring eastward, with the armored divisions in the lead and the foot infantry following to mop up stragglers. The prisoner haul was incredible, with the Third US Army taking in 68,192 prisoners from March 18 to 22 alone, while the Seventh US Army accounted for another 22,000. Thus, in clearing the Saar-Palatinate Triangle, the two American armies had eliminated over 100,000 of the enemy. These heady days can be summed up by an incident recorded by a XII Corps artillery officer, Captain Roland Jensen, who encountered an American soldier calmly fishing in a pond. "Hey!" yelled the captain. "Don't you know there's enemy around here?" The soldier replied, "No, it's safe enough; we're way behind the Kraut lines" (Dyer 1947, March 21, 1945). Not to be outdone, Weyland's XIX TAC flew an incredible 714 sorties on March 18. But it was on March 19 that his pilots flew one of the more memorable missions of the war.

Airstrike on Ziegenberg Castle, March 19, 1945

On March 18, Weyland's team received reliable confirmation that Kesselring's OB West was situated in Ziegenberg Castle, about 10km west of Bad Nauheim. Immediately nearby was Hitler's Adlerhorst, or Eagle's Nest, a headquarters complex built by Albert Speer in 1940. It was at Rundstedt's OB West in Ziegenberg that the German generals had been rallied for their briefing, at the Adlerhorst, just before the Ardennes Offensive. Ensconced in rugged terrain on a wooded hill, the castle was well protected by security and antiaircraft guns. The staff typically handled day-to-day operations on the lower floors and in several bunkers nearby, but took their meals and spent relaxation time on the upper levels and in the castle grounds.

Set out in Weyland's Field Order No. 234, the mission was to strike the headquarters with an all-out effort by Colonel Edwin Chickering's 367th Fighter Group. Even as they planned the attack for the next day, Reichsminister Albert Speer was road-bound from Berlin, traveling at night so as to arrive the next morning to meet with Kesselring to discuss one of Hitler's recently released scorched-earth decrees. He was scheduled to meet with the field marshal during lunch, which was the same time the 367th planned to make their attack so as to maximize effect. The 394th Fighter Squadron, with 16 P-47s led by Major Charles Matheson, was to make the initial low-level attack, but ground fog obscured the target and his planes flew along the wrong valley near the target. However, Lieutenant Allen Diefendorf, leading 16 P-47s of the 392nd Fighter Squadron, spotted the castle from 7,000ft and made a diving attack on it. The time was 1335hrs, just minutes after the Germans started lunch. Diefendorf, along with his wingman Captain John C. Adams, led the attack from the east.

Kesselring was just finishing a toast he had proposed to celebrate Speer's 40th birthday, when the guests heard the screaming whine of approaching aircraft. A few just had time to see the red noses of the incoming Thunderbolts as the windows were shattered by the .50-caliber slugs. Diefendorf placed his two 1,000lb bombs directly into the front doors and then yanked up on the stick, barely clearing the castle tower. The bombs came in rapid succession, each with a delay fuse to ensure penetration of the structure. The German officers rushed for the tunnels and to the bunkers even as Kesselring took a blow to the head from a falling chandelier. As Diefendorf's Thunderbolts peeled away, Matheson's pilots now identified the target and banked in to make their own attack. The southeasternmost wing of the castle, which included Kesselring's quarters and study, was blown apart, as were adjacent structures. But the 367th was not done, for Major Chester Slingerland, leading 16 P-47s of the 393rd Fighter Squadron and loaded with napalm, now made his run. Over 75 percent of the castle, along with several other buildings, was both blasted and burned out. The resulting devastation and casualties disrupted the headquarters at a critical moment and added insult to injury to the German war machine, for not even their most senior headquarters in the West were secure from attack. However, Chickering's

Patton with Bradley and Brigadier-General Otto P. Weyland (center), commander of XIX Tactical Air Command. Weyland's fighter-bombers raked over the battlefield in a brutal display of combat aviation that resulted in smashed German columns during their retreat to the Rhine. It was Weyland's aircraft that attacked Kesselring's OB West headquarters at Ziegenberg on March 19, 1945, using both high-explosives and napalm to burn out the castle and adjacent buildings. (US Army Signal Corps/The General George Patton Museum)

367TH FIGHTER GROUP AIRSTRIKE ON ZIEGENBERG CASTLE, MARCH 19, 1945 (PP. 52–53)

On March 19, 1945, the P-47s of the 367th Fighter Group, composed of the 392nd, 393rd, and 394th Fighter squadrons, attacked Kesselring's Oberbefehlshaber (OB) West headquarters at Ziegenberg Castle (right next to Hitler's Adlerhorst). The 367th was one of the fighter groups that was part of the XIX Tactical Air Command, which provided direct support to Patton's Third Army. The P-47s struck the target with both high-explosives and napalm.

Lieutenant Al Diefendorf, the assistant flight commander for C Flight, 392nd Fighter Squadron, was detailed to lead his squadron's attack on Ziegenberg castle. Diefendorf spotted the castle from 7,000ft, after Major Charles Matheson's 394th Fighter Squadron, slated to lead the attack, was confused by low-lying haze and turned up the wrong valley.

Colonel Chickering, commander of the 367th Fighter Group and in charge of the entire mission, gave Diefendorf the go-ahead to alter the original plan and launch the attack. "Hit it!" Chickering called out over the radio. The time was 1335hrs.

Inside the castle, Field Marshall Albert Kesselring was proposing a birthday toast to his distinguished visitor, Armaments Minister Albert Speer, when they heard the approaching planes.

This scene shows the 392nd Fighter Squadron being led in to the attack by Diefendorf (1) and his wingman Captain John C. Adams (2). Diefendorf has squeezed the trigger on his yoke to unleash .50-caliber slugs from his eight machine guns, so as to start his gun camera and film the attack. Both he and Adams have dropped a pair of 1,000lb general-purpose bombs (3), each set with delay fuzes so as to maximize penetration. Diefendorf's bombs have penetrated the front doors and explode within the palace of the castle. His P-47 has barely cleared the castle tower.

Between he and his wingman, close to 30 German staff officers and other personnel will be killed in the initial attack.

Kesselring, Speer, and their staffs began to flee through the exploding structure to bunkers below and to the north side of the palace (4). The explosions came seconds apart as each P-47 from the 392nd made its pass. Speer escaped injury, but Kesselring received a minor head wound from a falling chandelier.

Having corrected his error, Major Matheson brought the 394th in for another attack, dropping a further round of 1,000lb bombs on the castle, the outer buildings to the north, and the town of Ziegenberg. Only a single German light antiaircraft gun engaged the incoming aircraft, and a strafing run quickly silenced it. Altogether, Matheson's pilots and the 392nd delivered 60 1,000lb bombs on the target.

At 1355hrs, the 393rd Fighter Squadron, under Major Chester Slingerland and loaded with napalm, which was then still a relatively new weapon, banked in to make its attack. The intent was for the napalm to burn its way into any underground structures and kill personnel who survived the initial attack. Seven 150-gallon napalm containers hit the castle and two landed on the town. The flaming gel burned out the blasted structure, leaving most of the castle and nearby town destroyed. The staff and headquarters function for OB West was severely disrupted as a result.

All planes return undamaged, and the 367th Fighter Group received its second Distinguished Unit Citation for the mission. Patton later expressed his admiration for the accuracy of the pilots during the attack, and Rundstedt, though no longer in command at OB West, noted that such attacks made his heart troubles worse: "This is a hard life for an old soldier."

367th would be able to savor this triumph only briefly, for Slingerland, a popular leader with the pilots, would be killed in action four days later over Bad Kreuznach when his P-47 took a direct hit from an 88.[4]

Escape to the Rhine

By March 19, Felber's 7.Armee had largely ceased to exist. While fragments of units continued to infiltrate through the American lines toward the predesignated crossing sites of the Rhine at Mainz, Ludwigshafen, and Germersheim, they did so as fugitives. Caught in a vice in the vicinity of the town of Lauterecken, just southwest of Bad Kreuznach, were the remnants of four German divisions: 2.Panzer-Division and 9.Volksgrenadier-Division from Oriola's XIII.Armee-Korps, and 212.Volksgrenadier-Division and 352. Volksgrenadier-Division from LXXX.Armee-Korps, all now under Oriola's command. Even as Oriola attempted to rally these forces, he watched from his command post at Wickenrodt an American armor attack develop and overrun his 9.Volksgrenadier-Division and Kampfgruppe Buddenbrock, which had been formed to protect the corps's right flank. He noted that American tanks avoided the roads, instead clinging to the high ground so as to pour fire into the scattered German positions manning the feeble roadblocks in the valleys.

Most of the forces in the Lauterecken pocket would be wiped out over the next few days, with the few elements that trickled eastward being reformed under the command of Generalleutnant Franz Sensfuss of 212.Volksgrenadier-Division. Lauchert and a few of his staff from 2.Panzer-Division, being younger and more physically fit than many of their counterparts, managed to work their way to the Rhine. To continue their escape, they swam the river, which was no small feat. The few cadre remaining of this once-famous division were withdrawn to Thuringia to be reformed into a *Kampfgruppe*.

Even as Felber's command seemed to disappear before his eyes, two divisions had at last begun to arrive in an effort to stem the American juggernaut. Both 47.Volksgrenadier-Division and 559.Volksgrenadier-Division had been delayed by the incessant American air attacks, but at last 47.Volksgrenadier-Division, commanded by Generalleutnant Max Bork, began to gradually deploy into the Alzey area, just in time to take the full force of the 4th Armored Division's ongoing assault. Gaffey's unit, having first been oriented toward Mainz in the hope of finding an intact bridge, was then turned toward Worms, which air reconnaissance confirmed was the location of the last intact bridge over the Rhine in that area.

Having brought his division north from Alsace, Bork was attempting to set up a delaying action on the fly with Worms as the pivot point. While an element of his division, along with modest tank support, had launched a counterattack on the 18th, Bork's efforts were bedeviled by the collapse of LXXX.Armee-

A typical view of a developing American tank attack, conditions similar to what Generalleutnant Max Bork, commander of the German 47.Volksgrenadier-Division would have experienced when trying to block the 4th Armored Division's movement toward Worms. Formations would move dispersed to not present themselves as concentrated targets for both artillery and antitank fire, and an armored recovery vehicle typically followed, prepared to rescue bogged down or damaged vehicles. (US Army Signal Corps/The General George Patton Museum)

4   Richard Groh, *The Dynamite Gang: The 367th Fighter Group in World War II*, Fallbrook, CA: Aero Publishers, Inc., 1983, pp. 135–43, and XIX Tactical Air Command, *Tactical Air Operations in Europe: A Report on the Employment of the XIX TAC, 1 Aug 1944–9 May 1945*.

THIRD US ARMY
1. Third US Army HQ (Lieutenant-General George S. Patton, Jr.)
XII Corps
2. XII Corps HQ (Major-General Manton Eddy)
3. 5th Infantry Division (Major-General Leroy Irwin)
4. 4th Armored Division (Major-General Hugh Gaffey)
5. 11th Armored Division (Brigadier-General Charles Kilburn)
XX Corps
6. XX Corps HQ (Major-General Walton Walker)
7. 10th Armored Division (Major-General William Morris)
8. CCA, 10th Armored Division (Brigadier-General Edwin Pilburn)
9. CCB, 10th Armored Division (Colonel Basil Thayer; March 19, Colonel Thomas Brinkley)
10. 94th Infantry Division (Major-General Harry Malony)
11. 80th Infantry Division (Major-General Horrace McBride)
12. 26th Infantry Division (Major-General Willard Paul)
13. 12th Armored Division (Major-General Roderick Allen)
14. 65th Infantry Division (Major-General Stanley Reinhart)
SEVENTH US ARMY
15. Seventh Army HQ (Lieutenant-General Alexander Patch)
16. 70th Infantry Division (Major-General Allison Barnett)
17. 45th Infantry Division (Major-General Robert Frederick)
18. 6th Armored Division (Major-General Robert Grow)

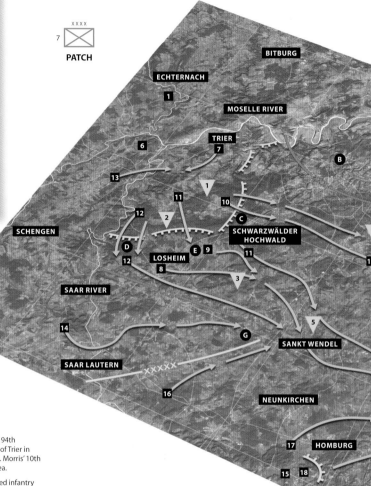

▼ EVENTS

1. As the XII Corps to the north crosses the Moselle, the 26th, 80th, and 94th Infantry divisions of Walker's XX Corps expand their lodgment south of Trier in preparation for offensive operations, during the period March 13–14. Morris' 10th Armored Division prepares for exploitation operations in the Trier area.

2. On March 15, the 10th Armored Division, with a regiment of motorized infantry in support, advances southeast passing through the 80th and 94th Infantry divisions. The strongest resistance is from SS-Gebirgsjäger-Regiment 12 under SS-Standartenführer Schreiber of 6.SS-Gebirgs-Division "Nord" in the area around Losheim. This resistance is largely bypassed.

3. Morris' tankers continue to avoid the SS troops, and by March 16 are ordered to advance on Kaiserslautern. The 10th Armored Division goes around resistance to concentrate on areas of German weakness, with CCB under Colonel Thayer advancing past the SS troops to the north while CCA under Brigadier-General Pilburn circles around their southern flank, with both combat commands striking for Sankt Wendel.

4. On March 17, Allen's 12th Armored Division joins in on the attack, moving on an axis in conjunction with the 94th Infantry Division, crossing the upper Nahe River south of Idar-Oberstein.

5. By March 18, the XX Corps has been reinforced to four infantry, two armored divisions and two cavalry groups, making it the most powerful ever employed by the Third US Army. During the day, the 10th Armored Division rolls through Sankt Wendel with virtually no opposition.

6. In Eddy's XII Corps to the north, the 4th Armored and 90th Infantry divisions resume their advance on March 18 toward the Mainz area, primarily in search of a bridge to cross the Rhine. Concurrently, the 11th Armored Division presses east to just north of Kaiserslautern, while the 10th Armored Division from Walker's corps moves around the southern environs of the city.

7. On March 19, Bork's 47.Volksgrenadier-Division begins to arrive in the area of Alzey in an attempt to stymie the drive of Eddy's XII Corps. Bork has to dodge the massed attack of hundreds of vehicles from Gaffey's 4th Armored Division as it drives southeast, descending into the flat river plain of the Rhine. The 4th Armored had been rerouted toward Worms in search of an intact bridge after

90th Infantry Division troops found the bridges at Mainz blown. Bork manages to withdraw most of his division to the Germersheim bridgehead 40km south of Ludwigshafen.

8. Mühlen's 559.Volksgrenadier-Division attempts to move northwest to assist 47.Volksgrenadier-Division, but its arrival is piecemeal. The division is routed and the remnants driven south toward the Germersheim bridgehead. All efforts to block the XII US Corps' advance east to the Rhine have to this point, on March 19, completely failed.

9. On March 20, the Third and Seventh US armies join hands near Kaiserslautern when Paul's 26th Infantry Division makes contact with Grow's 6th Armored Division. Kaiserslautern is occupied the next day with little fighting, most resistance being from snipers and poorly manned roadblocks.

10. On March 21, Worms is captured by elements of both the 11th and 4th Armored divisions, and the 12th Armored Division enters Ludwigshafen. Irwin's 5th Infantry Division also reaches the area of Oppenheim. Patton's Army is now firmly on the Rhine River, though so far, all bridges reached have been destroyed.

11. CCA of the 10th Armored Division probes down the main route toward Bad Durkheim and Neustadt-Weinstrasse. On March 22, the 13th Tank Battalion, supported by infantry from the 317th Regiment of the 80th Infantry Division, advances to Neustadt and engages in a duel with Jagdtigers of schwere Panzerjäger-Abteilung 653. This unit will engage in running gun battles with the 10th Armored over two days before withdrawing east across the Rhine, leaving behind several broken-down Jagdtigers.

THIRD US ARMY CONVERGES ON THE RHINE

The drive of US XX Corps east, imploding the growing pocket of both 7.Armee and 1.Armee, and reaching the Rhine River.

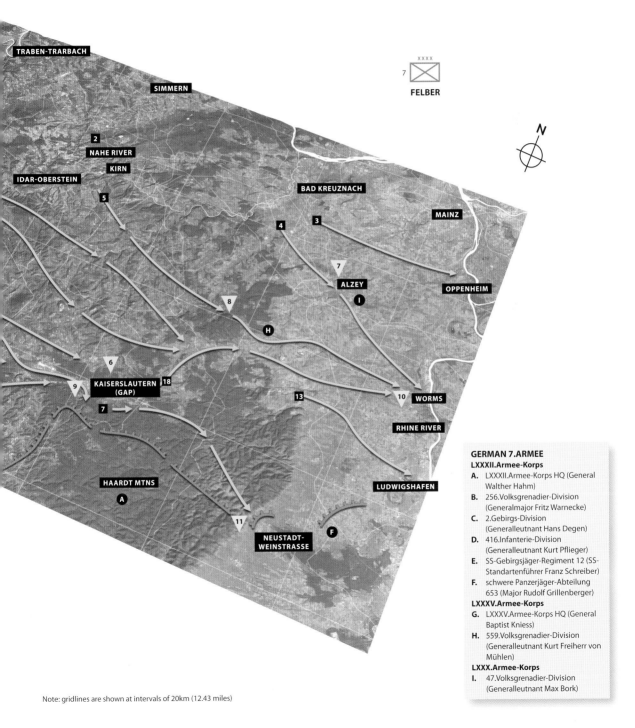

TRABEN-TRARBACH

SIMMERN

7 | XXXX | FELBER

2

NAHE RIVER

KIRN

IDAR-OBERSTEIN

5

BAD KREUZNACH

MAINZ

4 | 3

7

ALZEY

I

OPPENHEIM

8

H

6

9 | KAISERSLAUTERN (GAP) | 18

7

13

10 | WORMS

RHINE RIVER

LUDWIGSHAFEN

HAARDT MTNS

A

11

NEUSTADT-WEINSTRASSE

F

Note: gridlines are shown at intervals of 20km (12.43 miles)

GERMAN 7.ARMEE

LXXXII.Armee-Korps

A. LXXXII.Armee-Korps HQ (General Walther Hahm)

B. 256.Volksgrenadier-Division (Generalmajor Fritz Warnecke)

C. 2.Gebirgs-Division (Generalleutnant Hans Degen)

D. 416.Infanterie-Division (Generalleutnant Kurt Pflieger)

E. SS-Gebirgsjäger-Regiment 12 (SS-Standartenführer Franz Schreiber)

F. schwere Panzerjäger-Abteilung 653 (Major Rudolf Grillenberger)

LXXXV.Armee-Korps

G. LXXXV.Armee-Korps HQ (General Baptist Kniess)

H. 559.Volksgrenadier-Division (Generalleutnant Kurt Freiherr von Mühlen)

LXXX.Armee-Korps

I. 47.Volksgrenadier-Division (Generalleutnant Max Bork)

Men of the 302nd Infantry Regiment, 94th Infantry Division, engage possible enemy positions on the opposite side of the Rhine near Mannheim on March 21. At this point, German commanders were uncertain precisely where Patton would attempt to cross, but prioritized Mainz as the most dangerous possibility. The 94th Division was still fairly new to combat, having been severely tested at Trier when attacked by 6.SS-Gebirgs-Division "Nord." (NARA)

Korps to his south, being overrun by Dager's 11th Armored Division. With his command post at Grundheim, to the southeast of Alzey, Bork had an almost perfectly unobstructed view to the west and northwest, as the terrain gradually ascended west away from the Rhine. From there, on the afternoon of March 20, he watched in stunned fascination the rolling advance of the entire 4th Armored Division, with upwards of 200 tanks and half-tracks rumbling southeast toward Worms, cascading their way down the gentle slopes and through the nearby vineyards in what was the classic example of an armored division in action. Bork sped off to quickly make a personal reconnaissance of the Worms bridgehead, only to find that the local commander had abandoned his positions. Racing back to his division, he had to dodge American tank fire as he tried to get his division back to the Rhine.

The 559.Volksgrenadier-Division, under Generalleutnant Kurt Freiherr von Mühlen, had been Hausser's hope for some form of reserve, but the division had been holed up in a Siegfried Line position south of Saarbrücken, thus requiring Hitler's direct permission to pull it out. It was not until March 15 that two battalions of the division became available to Felber's 7.Armee. As it were, Mühler's division was arriving too little, too late, and was caught up in the ensuing rout southeast of Bad Kreuznach. By this point, any defensive measures by Heeresgruppe G and 7.Armee were, in the words of SS-Oberst-Gruppenführer Hausser, "solely improvisations" (European Theater Historical Interrogation B-600, p. 28). With communications in shambles, it was next to impossible to coordinate any type of serious countermeasures. These problems were exacerbated by air attacks against Felber's headquarters near Wachenheim on March 18, forcing the command group to displace a few kilometers east to Ellerstadt. Such repeated displacements by the command groups of all of the German headquarters only added to the overall disruption to operations.

THE RHINE CROSSING

By 21 March, both sides were in a full-blooded race for the Rhine, the Germans attempting to escape and the Americans in search of a bridge. On the previous day, Patton, along with Bradley, had another meeting with Devers and Patch to discuss coordination of actions along the new boundary. During the meeting, Patch wanted to wager a bet with Patton that his troops would be in Kaiserslautern before those of the Third US Army. Patton declined the bet politely, but without telling Patch that his 10th and 12th Armored divisions had already bypassed and then taken the city the day before.[5] By the next day, they were pushing hard for the Rhine.

Despite the speed of his advance, Patton was not going to leave his objective of breaching the river to chance. Since October of the previous year, he had squirreled away bridging equipment and Navy landing craft in France near Nancy. Since this assembly area was along the upper Moselle River, Patton's engineer units had been cycling through a series of training courses in preparation for a Rhine crossing. The engineers trained on handling various bridges, ferries, and the use of storm and assault boats, which used small outboard motors. The storm boats used a 55hp motor to provide sufficient speed to allow a small team, usually six infantry with two engineers to crew it, to beach the boat and quickly disembark. The assault boat carried a squad of eight with two engineers and was usually paddled, thus making it the boat of choice for a quiet night crossing. Some of the engineers already had a chance to put their schooling to use on both the Kyll and lower Moselle River crossings in February and March. Now, they were being called upon once more to breach the Rhine, the great river of myth and lore.

Patton had longed for the opportunity to cross the Rhine, and ensured his staff made adequate preparations to move boats and bridging equipment to the front. Here a column of Navy LCM landing craft are trucked forward through the village of Frei-Laubersheim, near Bad Kreuznach. LCMs were larger than LCVPs and could carry heavier loads, including light and medium tanks. Today, the road has been re-routed with a private home now located where the lead vehicle is standing. (NARA)

Since late 1944, Patton's engineers and staff had studied various Rhine River crossing sites and separated them into two zones, the first being between Bingen and Worms and the second between Cologne and Koblenz. The Germans had made similar studies prior to the war, and such places as Kaub and Nierstien–Oppenheim stood out, though there were other vulnerable crossing sites as well. Patton had already chosen the Nierstein–Oppenheim site, possibly even before the Normandy invasion, as one of the most likely points to cross, and thus his operational planning favored movements in that direction (Patton 1974, p. 661). The area offered a good road network and the terrain favored an attack from the west, with hills over 100m high dominating the flat eastern side.

Getting the equipment to the crossing site quickly was another problem. At the time, the remnants of 13 German divisions were still in the Saar-Palatinate Triangle, making it impractical to transport the materiel directly from Toul to the necessary location. Thus, they had to be routed north to follow the west bank of the Moselle River, and then move south in the wake of the 4th Armored Division's advance. Traffic control was of paramount importance, as each convoy of vehicles had to move at precise times to avoid a logjam of vehicles on the roads, which would make them ideal targets for German aircraft. While the Luftwaffe had been dormant early on and the XIX TAC ruled the skies, by the time Patton's troops were closing on the Rhine, German aircraft began to make more regular appearances over the battlefield. The first uptick in German aircraft arrived over the battlefield

---

5   March 20 diary entry of Brigadier-General Hobart Gay.

Two abandoned Jagdtigers in Neustadt from Leutnant Kasper Geoggler's team, being part of schwere Panzerjäger-Abteilung 653 under Major Rudolf Grillenberger. Geoggler's three Jagdtigers, along with replacement troops and local Volksturm, were to block the 10th Armored Division's advance toward the Rhine. While having initial success, two of his temperamental beasts broke down near the corner of what is today Landauer and Speyerdorfer streets, March 22. The farthest vehicle has its gun out of battery, the crew having drained the hydraulic fluid before firing a round and damaging the gun so that it could not be used by the enemy. (NARA)

on March 17, when the Third US Army reported nine raids of 47 aircraft. But by the 20th, the Luftwaffe threw in 314 aircraft on 61 separate raids, including jet-propelled Me 262s. Their targets included the columns of the 4th Armored and 90th Infantry divisions, and the bridging sites on the Nahe River. Gunners shot down 25 aircraft and claimed 11 more as probably destroyed. In addition, Weyland's pilots accounted for another eight. Nevertheless, columns of bridging equipment would present themselves as lucrative targets if not moved skillfully.

As Patton's divisions closed in on the Rhine, some of the weary Jagdtigers of Major Rudolf Grillenberger's schwere Panzerjäger-Abteilung 653 clattered into the picturesque town of Neustadt, situated on the famous Weinstrasse. To the west was the rugged Haardt Mountains, dotted with medieval castles; to the east, the open plains leading to the river. Grillenberger had with him about 30 operational vehicles, but only a handful were truly combat ready after having endured weeks of uninterrupted action in the Wissembourg Gap. At 70 tons, the Jagdtiger was the heaviest combat vehicle fielded by either side, with both heavy armor and a powerful 128mm gun. However, it was grossly underpowered and suffered teething mechanical problems.

Grillenberger's mission on March 21 was to block a further advance of American forces toward the southeast, in order to protect the German bridgehead at Germersheim and allow 18 of his damaged tank destroyers to be evacuated by rail across the river. The major dispersed what he had left, comprising three Jagdtigers and a few half-tracks under Leutnant Kasper Geoggler, to take up position on the high ground north of Neustadt so as to cover the main approach route coming from the west. The rest were distributed in the plain to the east. Geoggler's vehicles were not alone, being supported by a motley collection of local Volksturm and a handful of determined replacement troops and flak gunners.

In the early morning hours of March 22, CCA of the 10th Armored Division under the command of Brigadier-General Edwin Pilburn, was probing its way into Neustadt, with Lieutenant-Colonel Henry Cherry's 3rd Tank Battalion in the lead, in particular B Company under 1st Lieutenant Barnes. Supporting Barnes' Combat Team was a battalion of infantry from the 80th Division's 317th Regiment. After shooting up a German supply column near Frankenstein, in what Patton remarked as "the greatest scene of carnage I have ever witnessed" (Codman 1957, p. 268), the team pushed toward Neustadt in the early morning dark only to take fire from Geoggler's Jagdtigers. While the Germans claimed 25 tank destroyers and tanks knocked out, the American after-action reports indicated that only a few were actually destroyed. Nevertheless, this action stalled the American advance, allowing Geoggler to move his giant machines off the vineyard-covered slopes and into the town itself.

The Americans resumed their advance, only to find Neustadt to be a hotbed of bazooka and sniper fire. The latter was most troublesome, and a number of officers were hit, including Cherry and Barnes, the latter mortally wounded. The Jagdtigers positioned themselves to the east side of the town, with one oriented to guard the main road. They knocked out several vehicles before withdrawing, leaving behind two of their own Jagdtigers when they broke down. Concurrently, in the nearby town of Böhl, Grillenberger's other Jagdtigers knocked out almost a dozen tanks and half-tracks. With their mission accomplished, the battalion withdrew to the east and crossed the Rhine at Germersheim on March 24, though having only modestly delayed the American advance. By this point, most of the Jagdtigers were in desperate need of two weeks of maintenance, and most had to be evacuated to their new depot location west of Stuttgart for repair.

Fragments of other units preceded schwere Panzerjäger-Abteilung 653 across the river, including the remnants of Oriola's corps and Bürcky's 159. Volksgrenadier-Division. The 17.SS-Panzergrenadier-Division "Götz von Berlichingen" was so beat up that it had to be pulled to the rear for complete refitting. By March 21, Felber's 7.Armee had been relieved of all responsibility for units still west of the Rhine, this being assumed by Förtsch's 1.Armee. Felber's task now was to reassemble what was left of his army and defend the Rhine from Wiesbaden to Mannheim, an area longer than what he had to defend on the Moselle, and now with virtually nothing to hand. At this point, the desperate plans previously laid to actuate the resources of the *Wehrkreise* system were put in full motion, and Wehrkreis XII in Wiesbaden, commanded by General Herbert Osterkamp became a de facto corps subordinated to Felber, joining the only other one he now controlled, Oriola's XIII. By now, both LXXXIX.Armee-Korps and LXXX. Armee-Korps had been detached to 15.Armee in the north and 1.Armee in the south respectively.

On March 22, the 10th Armored Division got to see the handiwork of either Weyland's fighter-bombers or the advancing tanks of the 13th Tank Battalion, the latter of which shot up a large German column on the road near the town of Frankenstein. This column was destroyed to the west of Bad Durkheim, and could very well have been the same smashed column that Patton saw, remarking that it was "the greatest scene of carnage I have ever witnessed." (NARA)

SCHWERE PANZERJÄGER-ABTEILUNG 653 JAGDTIGERS PREPARE TO ENGAGE THE 3RD TANK BATTALION (10TH ARMORED DIVISION) IN NEUSTADT, MARCH 22, 1945 (PP. 62–63)

Major Rudolf Grillenberger's schwere Panzerjäger-Abteilung 653, having been in action in northern Alsace, was called north to stem Patton's drive through the Palatinate. They had to road-march almost 100km, in vehicles already mechanically strained. Grillenberger was compelled to spread what serviceable vehicles he had across a wide area of the Rhine River basin.

Grillenberger ordered Leutnant Kasper Geoggler to block the road from Frankenstein to Neustadt so as to prevent the US Army's 10th Armored Division from penetrating into the Rhine basin and threatening the German bridgehead and escape route east at Germersheim. Even as Geoggler moved into Neustadt, CCA under Brigadier-General Edwin Pilburn was bearing down on them from the northwest, rolling down a highway through the rugged countryside in the dark.

Leutnant Geoggler, with only three Jagdtigers and some supporting infantry from a replacement battalion, flak gunners, and local Volksturm, took up a position on the vine-covered slopes north of Neustadt so as to have an excellent field of fire. In the early morning hours of March 22, the initial advance of the 10th Armored Division's 3rd Tank Battalion, under Lieutenant-Colonel Henry Cherry was stopped, with the loss of a number of tanks and tank destroyers. Leutnant Geoggler then repositioned his Jagdtigers to cover the main road through Neustadt and on the east side of the town.

This scene shows two of Grillenberger's Jagdtigers —nos. 331 and 323 (**1**, and **2**)— as they take up positions in the picturesque town of Neustadt. No. 331 is being oriented to guard an approach road, while No. 332 is positioned facing it, and will be hidden in bushes. Replacement infantry and Volksturm armed with panzerfausts (**3**), sniper rifles (**4**), and other personal weapons support the heavy tank destroyers, and are dispersing into the buildings. To orient the massive vehicles, the crews have to carefully ground guide them into firing positions so as to not cause inadvertent damage to the engines or suspension, even as they search for adequate fields of fire.

In late morning, the Americans resumed their advance. Tanks of the 3rd Tank Battalion, with 1st Lieutenant Barnes' B Company in the lead, pushed down the main street of Neustadt in search of their elusive enemy. They were delayed considerably by sniper and Panzerfaust fire from the buildings, the former proving particularly effective as snipers seriously wounded Cherry and killed several other armor leaders (including Barnes) as they rode in the open hatches of their tanks. The Americans, after losing a few more tanks to the Jagdtigers, probed down side streets to avoid them. Geoggler attempted to maneuver his vehicles, and two of them broke down at once. Unable to extricate them, the crews of one managed to drain the recoil fluid from the main gun before firing it to knock it permanently out of battery, and thus deny its use to the Americans. With one remaining Jagdtiger, Geoggler withdrew his team, having succeeded sufficiently in delaying the Americans and protecting the Germersheim bridgehead long enough for German forces in the area to withdraw to the east bank of the Rhine. It also allowed Grillenberger to save 18 of his damaged Jagdtigers from being captured or destroyed.

After the war, Jagdtiger No. 331 would be taken back to the USA, to Aberdeen Proving Grounds. It is one of only three surviving Jagdtigers.

The decision to start fully mobilizing Wehrkreis formations to fight in combat was in many ways the ultimate sign that the end was near. The Wehrkreis organizations were the foundation for the entire Wehrmacht, providing replacements, specialized training, officer and noncommissioned officer schools, hospital and veterinarian facilities, moral and welfare services, and even a military library and bookstore. Personnel assigned were usually combat veterans of extensive experience but who were no longer physically fit for front-line service. While elements of Wehrkreis XII had already been engaged in direct combat, the decision had not yet been made to fully mobilize it. But now, the full action plan of Wehrkreis XII was put into effect, and part of the plan was to divide the defense of the Rhine into three combat zones. The north was overseen by General Kurt von Berg, the center under General Siegfried Runge, and the south led by General Konrad von Alberti. Runge's and Alberti's sectors were in the zone of Felber's army, and thus came under his control.

On March 21, Felber took stock of what he had left, as he settled into his new headquarters site at Bensheim, along the Bergstrasse. To the south, he had his best formation, the 559.Volksgrenadier-Division holding around Ludwigshafen. Along with this unit he had the recently activated 172.Reserve-Division, a formation of various Wehrkreis XII replacement battalions and companies under Generalleutnant Hans Bölsen, that was holding the Ludwigshafen bridgehead. To the south of Ludwigshafen was Kampfbereich (Combat Zone) Süd under Alberti, which covered a sector from south of Worms to just north of Karlsruhe. To the north was Kampfbereich Mitte's

For the Third US Army, the German POW haul during the campaign was massive, with these captured by the 90th Infantry Division in Mainz on March 22 being just a small fraction of the tens of thousand brought in. German commanders were naturally upset that many of their troops would readily surrender to the Americans, in contrast to the Eastern Front, where the fear of Soviet captivity was high. Yet, some units with more enterprising leaders would attempt to infiltrate through the rapidly moving American units to reassemble once more on a preselected line of defense. (NARA)

Tanks of the 11th Armored Division enter the city of Worms on March 21, this portion being in far better condition than most of the city, which had been recently blasted by British and American air raids. This moment represented the second time the division had reached the Rhine River, having done so previously near Andernach. The soldier along the side of the road is probably part of an advance team to ensure the unit is directed to the right location. (US Army Signal Corps/The General George Patton Museum)

The 11th Armored Division reached the Rhine twice, first by Andernach near Koblenz and next when rolling into the ruins of Worms about one week later. This crew of the 41st Tank Battalion was cited as the first tank to reach the river during the breakthrough to Worms on March 21. The tank is a late-model M4A3 with the horizontal volute suspension system, which provided a smoother ride and better flotation in mud and snow. (NARA)

scratch forces under Runge, which was responsible for the sector from Wiesbaden to Gernsheim, southwest of Darmstadt, a defensive front of 40km. Most of Runge's formation, particularly the students and cadre of the local noncommissioned officer's school, was still assembling in the area of Rüsselsheim.

It was the sector facing west from Darmstadt that gave Runge and Felber the most serious cause for concern, for the only forces available were fragments of replacement and service units, supplemented by weak Volksturm battalions placed under Runge's command. One of these units was the remains of the Panzergrenadier-Ersatz- und Ausbildungs-Bataillon 104 from Landau, which had escaped from the west and found its way to the Gross-Gerau area opposite Oppenheim. Its prior responsibilities had been to generate replacements for 15.Panzergrenadier-Division, the inheritors of 15.Panzer-Division of Afrika Korps fame. Now, with a handful of other understrength replacement units and stragglers, they were thinly spread between Trebur and Riedstadt. In their desperation, they had press-ganged local civilians to assist, and when some refused, they were shot by Nazi officials. For a reserve, Felber could only count on the badly battered 159.Volksgrenadier-Division, fielding but two weak infantry regiments of a few hundred men each, and two batteries of 75mm guns. North of the Main River and not under Felber's control was a *Kampfgruppe* defending Frankfurt, along with the assembling elements of 198.Infanterie-Division under Generalmajor Konrad Barde, and 6.SS-Gebirgs-Division "Nord."

The German assessment considered Mainz the most obvious point for a crossing, as it channeled a railroad that would be needed to extend American supply lines eastward. The Oppenheim area was also considered; indeed, it had been assessed as an important crossing point in exercises before the war. However, with limited resources and time, Hausser and Felber had to make a choice and accept such a risk. They would have to protect Mainz as the most dangerous enemy course of action and hope that Patton would make the obvious choice. At the immediate moment, they had nothing but local Volksturm and security companies to hold the city.

On the west side of the Rhine, Eddy's XII Corps was racing up to the river. The 90th Infantry Division, having swept down the western bank of the Rhine from Boppard to Bingen, was now closing in on Mainz. The 4th Armored Division, having made its spectacular cross-country assault to Worms only to find its bridge over the Rhine destroyed, had now been routed north to the Oppenheim area, where Lieutenant-Colonel Irzyk's men took the opportunity to shoot up small river craft moored on the river. Meanwhile, the 11th Armored Division continued on to Worms, entering the ruined city on March 21. Irwin's 5th Infantry Division boys had pushed up close to the Rhine immediately behind the 4th Armored tankers. They were tired and badly in need of a rest, having been in action for several months.

On March 17, Patton's G-2 section under Colonel Oscar Koch warned him that a Panzer division—in this case, 11.Panzer-Division—was disengaging from the Remagen bridgehead and moving south. A few days later, Koch warned that another Panzer division was reforming east of the Rhine, and that another four divisions could reach the area in three days. This meant that any delay in crossing the river would meet with growing resistance. In Patton's thinking the solution was simple. He had to bounce the Rhine at once, and not later. Naturally, this fit well into his intentions of beating Montgomery's crossing, as the British field marshal's Operation *Plunder* was not to start until the night of March 23. But only if Patton moved quickly. Historians agree that Patton had his flaws, but lack of decision and speed was not one of them.

On March 21, Patton contacted Eddy and ordered him to ready the 5th Infantry Division to make an immediate crossing of the Rhine. This was not a total surprise, as Patton had already issued a warning order to XII Corps on March 19 to cross the Rhine in three days, and some crossing equipment was already being moved forward. But it was a surprise to Irwin, who was just briefing his staff that morning that they were to pull out of the line for a rest when he was told to report to Eddy's command post at once. At 1030hrs, Irwin learned that his division, having crossed 22 rivers in France and Germany, were now to conquer the greatest river in Europe, and on the fly no less. He considered such a venture as too risky, but conceded that he could get some kind of bridgehead established if needed, admitting in his diary (in the entry of 21 March) that, "it is a big and difficult operation,

Men of the 359th Infantry Regiment of Major-General Herbert Earnest's 90th Infantry Division, supported by an M10 of the 773rd Tank Destroyer Battalion, flush out a German pillbox in Mainz, March 22. By this point, much of the work in the city consisted of mopping up, with snipers and lone Panzerfaust gunners, so-called *Einzelkämpferen*, proving to be an annoying yet at times deadly problem. The 359th would soon join the rest of its division in crossing the Rhine. (NARA)

The Stinson L-5 Sentinel was one of the principle liaison aircraft used by the US Army. Nicknamed "Puddle Jumpers" and "Maytag Messerschmidts" by the troops, Patton's senior artillery officer, Brigadier-General Edward T. Williams, suggested using these aircraft to lift some of the 5th Infantry Division troops across the Rhine in what would have been the first airmobile operation in history. Though one company demonstrated the idea was feasible, it was scrapped when the amphibious landing came off successfully. (Universal History Archive/ Universal Images Group via Getty Images)

Nierstein–Oppenheim crossing, March 23–24, 1945

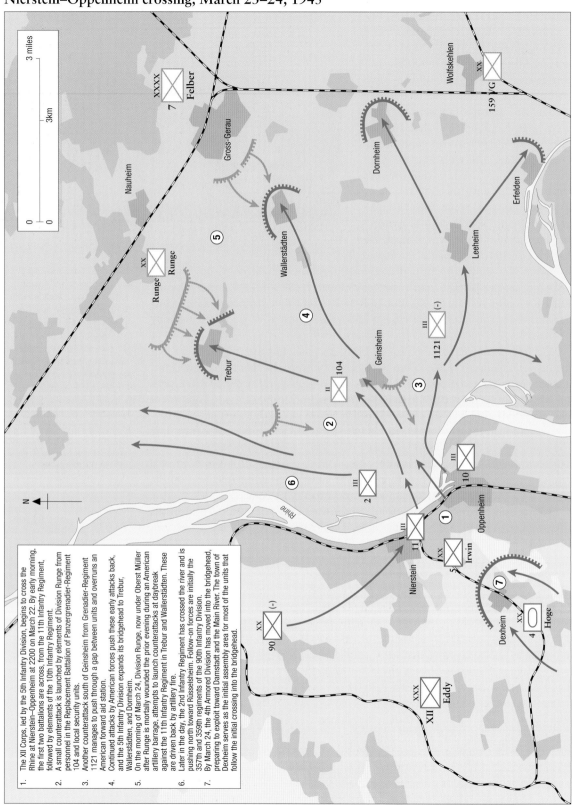

1. The XII Corps, led by the 5th Infantry Division, begins to cross the Rhine at Nierstein–Oppenheim at 2200 on March 22. By early morning, the first two battalions are across, from the 11th Infantry Regiment, followed by elements of the 10th Infantry Regiment.
2. A small counterattack is launched by elements of Division Runge from personnel in the Replacement Battalion of Panzergrenadier-Regiment 104 and local security units.
3. Another counterattack south of Geinsheim from Grenadier-Regiment 1121 manages to push through a gap between units and overruns an American forward aid station.
4. Continued attacks by American forces push these early attacks back, and the 5th Infantry Division expands its bridgehead to Trebur, Wallerstädten, and Dornheim.
5. On the morning of March 24, Division Runge, now under Oberst Müller after Runge is mortally wounded the prior evening during an American artillery barrage, attempts to launch counterattacks at daybreak against the 11th Infantry Regiment in Trebur and Wallerstädten. These are driven back by artillery fire.
6. Later in the day, the 2nd Infantry Regiment has crossed the river and is pushing north toward Rüsselsheim. Follow-on forces are initially the 357th and 359th regiments of the 90th Infantry Division.
7. By March 24, the 4th Armored Division has moved into the bridgehead, preparing to exploit toward Darmstadt and the Main River. The town of Dexheim serves as the initial assembly area for most of the units that follow the initial crossing into the bridgehead.

however, and it is hard to predict the outcome at this time." To support the crossing with a feint, the 2nd Cavalry Group under Colonel Charles H. Reed would finish clearing Mainz, supported by elements of the 90th Infantry Division.

Irwin's division took over the zone of the 4th Armored, allowing the tankers to organize and conduct badly needed maintenance on their vehicles. Even as he prepared his division and readied Colonel Paul Black's 11th Regiment to lead the crossing, a mass of equipment of all types descended on the area, assembling largely around the town

of Dexheim west of Oppenheim, and thus out of immediate observation from the east bank. Among the items being assembled were the Duplex Drive (DD) M-4 tanks of the 748th Tank Battalion. This unit had been far to the rear and had road-marched a significant distance to have at least some of their tanks arrive on time to provide amphibious tank support. With frantic preparations ongoing, Eddy's XII Corps had now been reinforced to five divisions: the 4th and 11th Armored, and the 5th, 26th, and 90th Infantry. But not one to view everything through a conventional lens, Patton was willing to entertain an interesting idea proffered by his chief artillery officer, Brigadier-General Edward T. Williams.

Among all the items of equipment within Third US Army were over 200 L-4 and L-5 light observation planes, what the troops called "puddle jumpers" and "Maytag Messerschmidts." The suggestion was to use a number of these to ferry troops across the river. Each plane could carry one fully loaded passenger, including essential heavy weapons like mortars and machine guns. It was assessed that an entire battalion could be flown over the river in several waves over a three-hour period. Patton loved the idea and ordered an immediate trial run, with C Company of Colonel Worrell Roffe's 2nd Regiment to try it out. By the afternoon of the 21st, repeated tests showed that the concept was indeed feasible, allowing a flexible option should the waterborne crossing run into trouble. The plan was later scrapped to the dismay of its proponents, largely because the water crossing succeeded and also because of increasing German air activity. Had it been implemented, it would have been the first airmobile operation in history.

March 22 arrived clear and unseasonably warm. The Rhine was surprisingly low considering the time of year, when it should have been significantly swollen with snow melt from the Alps, and the current was a modest 8km/h. Colonel Black was concerned about a lack of proper reconnaissance on the other side of the river, but believed the crossing could still be done. The 1st Battalion was slated to cross at Oppenheim, while the 3rd would cross at Nierstein. The initial wave would paddle over in M-2 assault boats, and once a foothold was established, the rest would follow in motorized boats. Eleven artillery battalions, ranging from 105mm to 8in. howitzers from both division and corps, were positioned to provide support,

By 0300hrs on March 23, Navy LCVPs began to rapidly move troops and jeeps across the river. Most combat reports referred to the light quarter-ton truck as a "peep," and it was not until near the end of the war that the word "jeep" became more popular. The landing site pictured is between Nierstein (in the background) and Oppenheim and was the location of the only immediate resistance faced by the crossing the previous night. Note the dead German in the foreground. (NARA)

While Patton's crossing proceeded to the south, units like the 76th Infantry Division lobbed artillery and mortar rounds over other parts of the river to the north to imply another crossing was imminent. Such feints proved vital in drawing away forces from the center of operations, and also allowed units to keep personnel focused through what amounted to on the job training when not employed in more direct action against the enemy. It was a common practice of commanders to keep soldiers busy with essential tasks even when it seemed to the average GI that the tasks were unnecessary. (NARA)

but unlike the Moselle crossing there would be no preparatory fires. Surprise was the essential ingredient. Having done all he could do to ready his division, Irwin went to bed at 2100hrs, one hour before the crossing was to start. Unable to sleep, he calmed his nerves with his favorite pastime, reading mystery novels.

The time had arrived. The moon was bright and virtual silence prevailed. It was 2200hrs, March 22, 1945. In his diary, Patton wrote that ever since closing up to the Rhine, he had wanted to get at least one battalion across, further noting that the Germans would not expect it because they were used to seeing massive build-ups before attempts were made to cross rivers. Company K of the 3rd Battalion, commanded by 1st Lieutenant Irven Jacobs, loaded up at Nierstein at 2215hrs and began to paddle quietly across the 800ft (240m) of the river. He and nine other men were the first to land on the opposite shore, with the rest of the company right behind them. They surprised seven Germans in a picket position, who promptly surrendered without a shot fired.

Additional companies began to cross, both at Nierstein and Oppenheim. It was at the latter that the first enemy shots rang out, and for a brief moment the regimental commander delayed further crossings. However, the 3rd Battalion pressed on. Just before 2230hrs, Irwin received a phone call at his bedside to tell him that the first two companies were across.

While the Nierstein crossing was easy, the most significant enemy resistance came at the Oppenheim site, with 1st Battalion troops taking both machine-gun and panzerfaust fire. The American infantrymen at times had to fire directly into German entrenchments to squelch the resistance, but soon

A mortar team and infantry from the 2nd Regiment, 5th Infantry Division board an LCVP for the trip across the Rhine at Nierstein, March 23. C Company of the 2nd Regiment was originally slated to cross the river via liaison aircraft in what would have been the first airmobile operation in history. The mission was cancelled when the amphibious part proved a success. (NARA)

after the landing the 1st Battalion began to press inland. The last machine-gun nest in the area was taken out by Private First Class Paul Conn, Jr., who at daylight came right at it with grenade in hand, causing the Germans to throw up their hands. By daylight, both battalions were firmly on the east bank and already pushing inland. Surprise had been so complete that ineffective German artillery fire did not start falling on the crossing sites until just after midnight, two hours after the crossing began. Moreover, as the 5th Infantry troops pressed inland, they caught many of the German troops sleeping in their quarters.

A Duplex Drive (or DD) tank from the 748th Tank Battalion enters the Rhine in support of the 5th Infantry Division. The DD tank's canvas screens were vulnerable to gunfire but their employment allowed for rapid armor support in the early stages of an amphibious operation. (Corbis via Getty Images)

Patton was beyond elated, noting in his diary entry of March 23 that "the 5th Division is over the Rhine. God be praised," adding that it was a "fitting climax to the preceding ten days." Patton's assessment could not have been more on the mark, for by smashing 7.Armee in the Saar-Palatinate, he had set the conditions to quickly bounce the Rhine. As Lieutenant-General Bradley finished his second cup of coffee at breakfast time, Patton telephoned to tell him he had pushed a division across the river that night. He only asked that Bradley keep it quiet for now to ensure he could hold the bridgehead. However, by that evening Patton phoned again to tell Bradley that he could shout it out to the world that he had beaten Montgomery across the Rhine. Having just received instructions from General Marshall, the US Army Chief of Staff, and Eisenhower that field commanders were to take greater pains to trumpet American combat successes, Bradley was more than willing to hold a press conference, "sticking the needle in Monty" regarding both American Rhine River crossings at Remagen and Oppenheim (Bradley 1999, p. 412).

While the Germans were tactically surprised, their response was weak in large measure because Felber had little in the vicinity of the bridgehead. As soon as he was aware of the crossing, he alerted Bürcky to get his depleted division on the move. In addition, he bolstered Bürcky's division by assigning to him Runge's *Kampfgruppe* and the students of a reserve officer's candidate school under Oberst Gerhard Kentner. The 159.Volksgrenadier-Division was reassembling just south of Darmstadt, while Runge's *Kampfgruppe* was thinly stretched along the river and Kentner's men were being assembled

An M36 Jackson of the 803rd Tank Destroyer Battalion supporting the 5th Infantry Division is ferried across the Rhine at Oppenheim, March 23. During any water crossing operation it was critical to get armor to the opposite bank as quickly as possible. LCVPs were too small to carry heavier vehicles, so these had to be ferried prior to the building of a bridge. Motorized assault boats were used to push the ferry across. The M36 was a further development of the M10 and mounted a highly effective 90mm gun. (NARA)

near Wiesbaden. Runge managed to scrounge six self-propelled guns from a local workshop, but he was still frantically trying to assemble whatever he could lay his hands on, including some convalescents from local hospitals as the Americans began to reinforce their bridgehead. Overall, Runge had approximately 5,000 men, only modestly equipped at best, with most of them assembled in the area of the Frankfurt airport.

In accordance with lessons learned, Bürcky intended to counterattack the bridgehead along both flanks, usually the weakest point in the early stages of a river crossing. The 159.Volksgrenadier-Division, recently reinforced by the rebuilt but orphaned Grenadier-Regiment 1121 formerly of 553. Volksgrenadier-Division, would attack from the southeast, while Runge's *Kampfgruppe* would attack from the north. Several small counterattacks had already been launched as early as first light on the 23rd, one of them by elements of Grenadier-Regiment 1121 south of Geinsheim that managed to penetrate the porous zone between American units and overrun a forward aid station. Though taking a number of prisoners, these were soon freed when the Americans drove the Germans back. In addition, some of Runge's security forces launched a sharp counterattack against the 3rd Battalion, 2nd Infantry Regiment at Trebur, which included at least several assault guns, and against the 1st Battalion, 11th Infantry Regiment at Wallerstädten. But, Felber pressed Bürcky to make a more concerted attack at once, despite the latter's opposition due to a lack of artillery. On the afternoon of March 23, the Germans launched their first coordinated counterattack against the bridgehead, but it was smashed before it barely started by a concentrated hail of steel from the American artillery on the opposite bank.

The Americans continued to reinforce the bridgehead. As early as 0300hrs, the LCVP Higgins boat drivers of Naval Unit 2 under the command of Lieutenant-Commander William Leide were already making plans, and before first light were steering their boats back and forth across the river. Initially, they had to beg for business, as too many of the infantrymen were still narrowly focused on trying to paddle their way across in the M-2 assault boats. However, by 0700hrs, Leide's men finally convinced the dogfaces to start using his boats, and soon 24 of these were rapidly making their runs. The Germans tried to drop artillery on them, but failed to make a single hit, and the crossing continued unabated, the landing craft soon joined by amphibious DUKWs, known to the troops as "Ducks," and M-28 tracked cargo carriers. Six DD tanks of the 748th Tank Battalion set up their canvas screens and slowly rolled into the water and swam to the opposite shore, and more armor from the 737th Tank Battalion, along with M-36 Jackson tank destroyers from the 803rd Tank Destroyer Battalion, followed on ferries.

The 1135th Engineer Group was the principle organization tasked with both deploying assault and storm boats and for building the bridges. On the morning of the 23rd, they began building the first two bridges, and within 36 hours both a heavy pontoon and treadway bridge were in operation. This stands in stark contrast to the lackadaisical approach to building additional bridges at the Remagen site, as it took the First US Army four days to complete their first bridge. Experience had already shown that one bridge does not a bridgehead make, and Patton's men applied this principle in spades. By late day of the 23rd, most of the 5th Infantry Division was across, along with two regiments of the 90th Infantry Division. The 90th's third regiment, the 358th, having just helped clear Mainz, was preparing to make their way over the bridges, as was the 4th Armored Division.

During the early evening hours, the American artillery continued to engage in sporadic fire missions at both clearly identified targets and key avenues of approach for enemy counterattacks. In the Gross-Gerau area, General Runge was trying to reorganize his *Kampgruppe* for another try at the bridgehead, having set up his headquarters in the cellar of a small forest house just east of the village of Königstadten. After a recent American artillery barrage in the area, Runge and several of his staff emerged to personally check on some of the preparations, only to be caught among the trees by another barrage. Runge was hit by a hot piece of shrapnel in the back and was evacuated to a field aid station in Nauheim, where he died shortly after. The last words of this Pour le Mérite and Knight's Cross holder were a fitting epitaph to the crumbling Reich: "There's nothing left to give." Runge's command was taken over by Colonel von Müller.

Almost 600km away in Berlin, the Oppenheim crossing was one of the subjects of the Führer conference that evening. Hitler assumed that the Rhine was breached at this point because the divisions of 1.Armee and 7.Armee

By March 24, a constant stream of traffic went both ways, with Third US Army vehicles crossing the completed bridge in the background and German prisoners being ferried across to the west bank. Many of the initial prisoners were captured while sleeping in dispersed quarters after the initial assault waves bypassed them. (NARA)

THIRD US ARMY

1. Third US Army HQ (Lieutenant-General George S. Patton, Jr.)

XII Corps
2. XII Corps HQ (Major-General Manton Eddy)
3. 5th Infantry Division (Major-General Leroy Irwin)
   2nd Infantry Regiment (Colonel Worrell A. Roffe)
   10th Infantry Regiment (Colonel Robert P. Bell)
   11th Infantry Regiment (Colonel Paul J. Black)
4. 90th Infantry Division (Major-General Herbert Earnest)
   357th Infantry Regiment (Colonel John H. Mason)
   358th Infantry Regiment (Colonel Jacob W. Bealke)
   359th Infantry Regiment (attached to 5th Infantry Division) (Colonel Raymond E. Bell)
5. 4th Armored Division (Brigadier-General William Hoge)
   (3 tank battalions; 3 infantry battalions; 3 artillery battalions)
   CCA (Colonel Hayden A. Sears)
   CCB (Lieutenant-Colonel Creighton W. Abrams)
   CCR (Colonel Wendell Blanchard)
6. 6th Armored Division (Major-General Robert Grow)
   (3 tank battalions; 3 infantry battalions; 3 artillery battalions)
   CCA (Colonel John L. Hines/Colonel Albert E. Harris)
   CCB (Colonel Harry F. Hanson)
   CCR (Colonel Albert E. Harris/Lieutenant-Colonel Embry D. Lagrew)
7. 26th Infantry Division (Major-General Willard Paul)
   101st Infantry Regiment (Colonel Walter T. Scott)
   104th Infantry Regiment (Colonel Ralph A. Palladino)
   328th Infantry Regiment (Colonel Aloysius E. O'Flaherty, Jr.)

XX Corps
8. XX Corps HQ (Major-General Walton Walker)
9. 80th Infantry Division (Major-General Horace McBride)
10. 11th Armored Division (Major-General Holmes E. Dager)

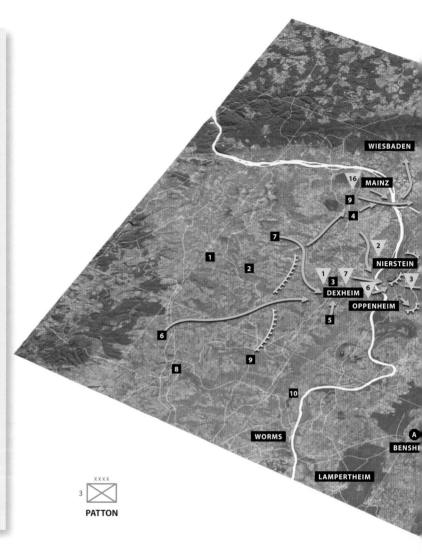

XXXX
3
PATTON

EVENTS

1. March 22: 1st and 3rd battalions of 11th Infantry Regiment, 5th Infantry Division assemble near Dexheim in daylight, preparing to cross the Rhine.

2. March 22, 2230hrs: 11th Infantry Regiment, 5th Infantry Division initiates the crossing at Nierstein and Oppenheim in small assault boats. By the end of the following day, the entire 5th Infantry Division plus two regiments of 90th Infantry Division are across.

3. March 23, early morning: Runge's Kampfbereich Mitte launches isolated and uncoordinated counterattacks against the new bridgehead, but these fail to slow the American advance.

4. March 23, afternoon: 159.Volksgrenadier-Division under Bürcky, and Reserve-Offizier-Bewerber (ROB) cadets from the officer candidate school in Wiesbaden under Oberst Gerhard Kentner, launch counterattacks on the northern side of the bridgehead around Trebur and Wallerstädten.

5. March 23, afternoon: While organizing his trooops, Runge is mortally wounded by a massive American artillery barrage on the woods east of Königstadten, where his headquarters is located.

6. March 23: US engineers of the 1135th Engineer Group throw two bridges across the Rhine at Nierstein and Oppenheim. The next morning, the rest of the 4th Armored Division begins to rapidly cross, followed by the remainder of the 90th Infantry Division. The Luftwaffe attempts to destroy the bridges, but air cover from Weyland's XIX TAC and local antiaircraft units keep the enemy aircraft at bay. Hoge's 4th Armored Division exploits eastward toward the Main River and Aschaffenburg, distracting the German commanders from Patton's true intent to exploit northeast.

7. Dexheim serves as the initial staging area for all units preparing to cross the Rhine.

8. The German 7.Armee commander, Felber, struggles to control the situation from his headquarters at Bensheim, south of Darmstadt. Direct control of the battle is taken from the Wehrkreis XII commander and given to General Baptist Kniess (LXXXV.Armee-Korps), who is replaced on March 31 by General Smilo Freiherr von Lüttwitz. Felber orders Darmstadt to be abandoned; Kesselring replaces him with General Hans von Obstfelder on March 25.

9. March 25: US 6th Armored Division crosses the Rhine and begins its exploitation to the northeast toward Frankfurt, supporting the advance of 5th Infantry Division. By March 25, Eddy's entire XII Corps is across the river.

10. Hausser and Obstfelder attempt to secure the Main River and destroy its bridges. Kleikamp's 36.Volksgrenadier-Division, as well as fragments of the 256. and 172. divisions, begin to assemble east and north of the Main. Division Nr. 413 under Generalleutnant von Schacky is dispatched westward by rail to assemble around Aschaffenburg.

11. March 25, evening: Irzyk's 8th Tank Battalion, 4th Armored Division manages to capture a partially intact bridge at Klein-Auheim. A firefight ensues with arriving 256.Volksgrenadier-Division troops around 2000hrs. The bridgehead is held.

12. March 25: German antiaircraft guns defending Frankfurt momentarily stall the American advance. Colonel Hines is seriously wounded at Mörfelden by an 88mm shell.

THE CROSSING OF THE RHINE

The exploitation of the Third US Army from the Rhine to the Main River, and the establishment of bridgeheads.

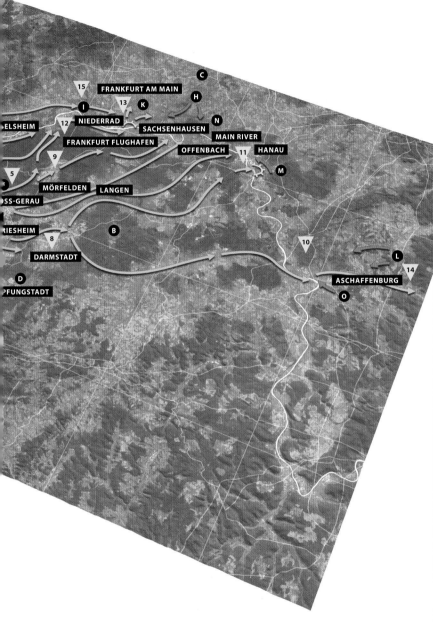

FELBER/ OBSTFELDER

GERMAN 7.ARMEE

A. 7.Armee HQ (General Hans Felber/Hans von Obstfelder on March 26)

B. Wehrkreis XII HQ (General Herbert Osterkamp)

C. LXXXV.Armee-Korps HQ (General Baptist Kniess/General Smilo Freiherr von Lüttwitz on March 31)

D. 159.Volksgrenadier-Division (Generalmajor Heinrich Bürcky); with Gruppe Stammberger; considered only marginally capable of defense

E. Reserve-Offizier-Bewerber Kentner (Oberst Gerhard Kentner); cadets from Wiesbaden Officer School, or officer applicants

F. Division Runge (General Siegfried Runge/ Oberst von Müller); scratch unit formed from river security and depot personnel, replacement units, convalescents

G. Volksgrenadier-Regiment 1121; detached from 553.Volksgrenadier-Division as of February 1945; commander unknown

H. 11.Panzer-Division (Generalleutnant Wend von Wietersheim)

I. 198.Volksgrenadier-Division (Generalmajor Konrad Barde)

J. 6.SS-Gebirgs-Division "Nord" (SS-Gruppenführer Karl Brenner); less elements

K. Kampfkommandant von Frankfurt/Main (Combat Commander Frankfurt/Main) (Generalmajor Friedrich Stemmermann—WIA March 27/Oberstleutnant Erich Löffler, KIA March 27)

L. 36.Volksgrenadier-Division (Generalmajor Helmut Kleikamp)

M. 256.Volksgrenadier-Division (Generalmajor Fritz Warnecke); only partially engaged

N. 172.Reserve-Division (Generalleutnant Hans Bölsen); largely from replacement and security personnel

O. Division Nr. 413 (Generalleutnant Siegmund Freiherr von Schacky auf Schönfeld); only marginally capable for defense; older personnel and antiquated equipment

13. March 26: Combat Team 9, 6th Armored Division captures a largely intact bridge over the Main River between Sachsenhausen and Frankfurt. By late afternoon, most of the 9th Armored Infantry Battalion has crossed the bridge into Frankfurt, followed later by troops from 11th Regiment, 5th Infantry Division. Oberstleutnant Löffler takes command of the Frankfurt garrison, but is mortally wounded a few hours later.

14. Patton orders a small task force under Captain Abraham Baum to drive deep into German-held territory to liberate American POWs at Oflag XIIIb, including his son-in-law, Lieutenant-Colonel John Waters, but the task force is cornered and destroyed.

15. March 26: Elements of Wietersheim's 11.Panzer-Division and 6.SS-Gebirgs-Division "Nord" begin to arrive in the Frankfurt area, but will be too late to prevent the fall of the city.

16. March 28: McBride's 80th Infantry Division forces the Rhine at Mainz and advances rapidly on Wiesbaden and Frankfurt, while the 5th Infantry and 6th Armored divisions advance from the south. Frankfurt falls on March 29.

had deserted the Siegfried Line. After exonerating Kesselring for the debacle, Hitler stated: "the worst thing is this second bridgehead here at Oppenheim. Is there still one of our panzer brigades or anything at all operating?" (Glantz and Heiber 2004, pp. 697–716). He was informed that 117 aircraft had been thrown at the bridgehead, including Me 262s, but that very few got through because they were intercepted by American planes. Later in the conference, Hitler expressed astonishment that the Americans got their bridging equipment to Oppenheim so quickly, and was then informed that other than five Jagdtigers at Sennelager, over 300km away, there was nothing to deploy against the bridgehead. When schwere Panzerjäger-Abteilung 653 was mentioned, Hitler also learned that it was currently engaged elsewhere and that Major Grillenberger was on the verge of being relieved, accused of tactical failure. But what truly stands out about these conferences was how much the Führer of the Third Reich was now meddling in the smallest of tactical minutia.

As March 24 arrived, the tempo accelerated rapidly and any German efforts to respond were once again too little, too late. Felber attempted to assemble additional scratch units to develop a defense in depth, and a few infantry divisions began to arrive between Frankfurt and Aschaffenburg, while even guards at the I.G. Farben plant in Ludwigshafen were pressed into action. Runge's division launched another attack against the Trebur area that morning, but it was repulsed by American artillery. In the meantime, Patton's engineers and MPs worked frantically, the former on building more bridges and the latter on controlling the traffic through all hours. Traffic control was so critical and overwhelming that even troops from an antitank battalion were pressed into service to keep men and vehicles moving. With the 5th Infantry Division completely across, Irwin's men had pushed east and to the north toward Rüsselsheim, thus shoring up the left flank. Simultaneously, the 4th Armored Division, now under Brigadier-General William M. Hoge of Remagen fame, had been assembling around the village of Dexheim. Combat Command A

began to cross the Nierstein bridge at 0900hrs, and were over just after lunchtime. Combat Command B followed at 1600hrs, and CCR by 2315hrs. The entire 4th Armored—amounting to 2,500 vehicles—was across in just 18 hours. Moreover, true to form Patton assigned the 104th Infantry Regiment of Paul's 26th Division to be motorized and attached to Hoge's tank units.

With the weather clear and warm, smoke generated by the chemical companies kept the bridges partly concealed in a haze, and pilots of the XIX TAC kept the Luftwaffe at bay, as the latter now tried desperately to interdict the crossing. Moreover, the engineers had erected three layers of defensive booms upstream across the river to prevent any boats loaded with explosives or frogmen from attacking the bridges. The Germans lobbed sporadic artillery fire at the site but to little effect; one 150mm round hit the first bridge but failed to explode. This bridge opened at 0130hrs on March 24, and was reinforced to Class 40 status in order to carry tanks by 0700hrs. A second bridge was opened by noon on March 25, with a third built shortly after. The rate of vehicle traffic was phenomenal, with the entire XII Corps of five divisions across by March 27, and over 60,000 vehicles crossing the bridges between March 24 and 31.

With the 4th Armored on the move, Patton and his aide Colonel Charles Codman arrived at the site of the Oppenheim bridge. As they walked across, he said halfway, "Time out for a short halt." After looking at the water flowing from under the bridge, he nonchalantly undid his trousers and urinated into the river, stating "I have been looking forward to this for a long time." Walking to the opposite bank, he stumbled and fell to one knee. But seizing the moment, he grabbed the churned earth with both hands and as he rose let it slide through his fingers. "Thus, William the Conqueror," he said. While Patton could be a showman, it was obvious that the men around him enjoyed the scene. Indeed, for Patton it was the culmination of his wildest dreams.

Probably, and unfortunately, the most memorable moment of Patton's Rhine crossing operation was when he urinated in the river on March 24. But while a number of different photos have surfaced purporting to be of the event, none have been determined to be of him actually engaged in the act. It would seem that the photos were taken after the fact, with Patton posing for the cameras. Regrettably, this understandable act of machismo, meant to highlight his dominance over the German war machine, would later overshadow the brilliant way in which Patton, his staff, and men conducted the entire campaign. (US Army Signal Corps/The General George Patton Museum)

EXPLOITATION: ON TO THE MAIN RIVER

The exploitation phase began almost at once, with the 4th Armored Division's CCA and CCB pushing through the lines of the 5th Infantry toward the southeast. They were met by only sporadic small-arms and panzerfaust fire, mostly from the 159.Volksgrenadier-Division, but also from a regiment of 352.Volksgrenadier-Division, which had just moved up on the right flank. Understrength and outgunned, they were pushed aside, prompting Bürcky to quickly evacuate his headquarters from the Pfungstadt area, though by this point his division had once more been virtually obliterated. In addition, the loss of much of the infantry in the area convinced Felber that he could not

Closing in on Frankfurt, March 25–26, 1945

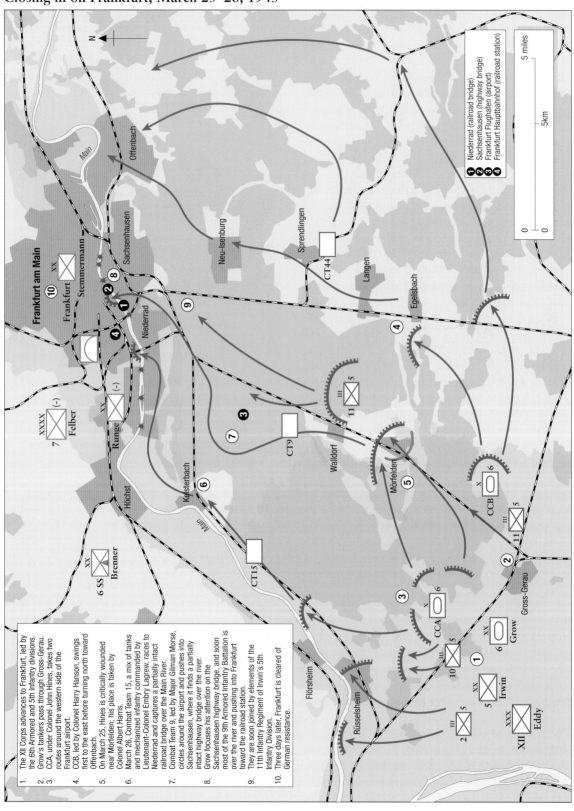

Legend:
- ❶ Niederrad (railroad bridge)
- ❷ Sachsenhausen (highway bridge)
- ❸ Frankfurt Flughafen (airport)
- ❹ Frankfurt Hauptbahnhof (railroad station)

Scale: 5 miles / 5 km

1. The XII Corps advances to Frankfurt, led by the 6th Armored and 5th Infantry divisions.
2. Grow's tankers pass through Gross-Gerau. CCA, under Colonel John Hines, takes two routes around the western side of the Frankfurt airport.
3. CCB, led by Colonel Harry Hanson, swings first to the east before turning north toward Offenbach.
4. On March 25, Hines is critically wounded near Mörfelden; his place is taken by Colonel Albert Harris.
5. March 26, Combat Team 15, a mix of tanks and mechanized infantry commanded by Lieutenant-Colonel Embry Lagrew, races to Niederrad and captures a partially intact railroad bridge over the Main River.
6. Combat Team 9, led by Major Gilman Morse, circles around the airport and pushes into Sachsenhausen, where it finds a partially intact highway bridge over the river.
7. Grow focuses his attention on the Sachsenhausen highway bridge, and soon most of the 9th Armored Infantry Battalion is over the river and pushing into Frankfurt toward the railroad station.
8. They are soon joined by elements of the 11th Infantry Regiment of Irwin's 5th Infantry Division.
9. Three days later, Frankfurt is cleared of German resistance.

Map labels: Main, Offenbach, Neu-Isenburg, Sprendlingen, Langen, Egelsbach, Frankfurt am Main, Frankfurt, Stemmermann, Sachsenhausen, Niederrad, CT44, Felber, Runge, Walldorf, CT9, Mörfelden, CCB, Höchst, Kelsterbach, 6 SS, Brenner, CT15, Gross-Gerau, Grow, CCA, Irwin, Flörsheim, Rüsselsheim, Eddy, XII

The famous German 88mm Flak 36 was their standard antiaircraft gun throughout the war. Many of these were pressed into service as artillery and for direct fire support and were deployed for ground combat during the American advance on Frankfurt. However, their cruciform mount and cumbersome mode of limbering and transportation limited their effectiveness and many were abandoned when enemy forces got too close. It was batteries of these types that caused Lieutenant-Colonel Albin Irzyk of the 4th Armored Division and Colonel John Hines of the 6th Armored Division significant difficulties. (NARA)

hold Darmstadt, and he ordered that the city be abandoned. This last decision was too much for Kesselring to accept, and he relieved Felber of command the next day, replacing him with General Hans von Obstfelder, who had been in command of 19.Armee further south. The Generalfeldmarschall's remarks to Felber that he was derelict in his duty demonstrated how far into fantasyland Kesselring had slid, a perspective that did not change even with his postwar memoirs. Wishful thinking could not change the catastrophe overtaking them; here there would be no triumph of the will.

On March 24, Major-General Robert W. Grow's 6th Armored Division, which had been until recently part of the Seventh US Army, was transferred to Eddy's XII Corps and assembled around Dexheim, with Colonel Harry Hanson's CCB moving into the bridgehead. By that time, another counterattack by German forces in the area, though achieving some initial success, was again smashed by concentrated artillery fire and caused little delay in the expansion of the bridgehead. The rest of Paul's 26th Infantry Division moved up along with McBride's 80th Infantry Division, and prepared to cross the river to backfill behind the lead units already across and pushing east. The 5th Infantry cleared Rüsselsheim and villages on the way to the Frankfurt airport, while elements of the 90th Infantry, in the form of Lieutenant-Colonel Frank Spiess' Task Force, along with parts of the 4th Armored Division, closed in on Darmstadt. By the end of the day, as Grow's tankers crossed the bridges in just 16 hours, the bridgehead was 14km deep and 16km wide. Darmstadt would be taken with only scant resistance the next day.

The German commanders on the spot, realizing that the Rhine was now irrevocably breached at this point, were hoping they could destroy the bridges over the Main River before those were lost. General Baptist Kniess' LXXXV.

Vehicles of CCA, 11th Armored Division, cross a pontoon bridge over the Main River at Gross-Auheim, near Hanau. While seizing an occasional bridge, most of Patton's troops crossed rivers like the Moselle, Rhine, and Main on pontoon and treadway bridges, with Patton's engineers performing feats of construction unheard of in most of the other field armies. Dager's 11th Armored Division was part of the follow-on pursuit into Germany. (US Army Signal Corps/The General George Patton Museum)

Armee-Korps headquarters was moved north to the Aschaffenburg–Hanau area, along with Generalmajor Helmut Kleikamp's 36.Volksgrenadier-Division and Generalmajor Fritz Warnecke's 256.Volksgrenadier-Division. Additionally, 172.Reserve-Division under Bölsen, absorbing the remnants of Runge's command, was moved north of the Main near Frankfurt and Hanau with the mission to collect stragglers and create a security line; and Division Nr. 413 led by Generalleutnant Siegmund Freiherr von Schacky auf Schönfeld was mobilized and sent west to deploy around the Aschaffenburg area. Schacky's division was poorly equipped and manned largely by battle-injured and older personnel who were not considered fit for combat action, with its commander describing his unit as no better than a pre-World War I formation. Orders were also given to accelerate the refitting of 17.SS-Panzergrenadier-Division "Götz von Berlichingen."

On March 25, CCA of the 4th Armored Division raced from the bridgehead, arriving at the Main River by Hanau and seizing a damaged but partly usable bridge by Klein-Auheim. Irzyk, whose battalion was again in the lead, had grabbed the bridge with C Company. Unable to get tanks across, Irzyk's armor took up firing positions on the west bank as the infantry from the 53rd Battalion pushed across and set up a bridgehead in Gross-Auheim. They had barely established themselves when at 2000hrs a fully loaded troop train, probably being elements of 256.Volksgrenadier-Division, rolled in from the south. A fierce firefight began, as the German troops piled from the cars and went immediately into action in the growing darkness. Despite being able to push back on the bridgehead, American artillery once again proved to be a deciding factor in stopping the German attack.

Despite the rapid advance, CCA was now hung up on the Main River through March 26, though it did manage to clean up areas on the west side of the river, which included the capture of a large warehouse with $2.5 million in medical supplies and 10,000 tires. CCB on the other hand had managed to capture an intact bridge south of Aschaffenburg on the afternoon of March 25, and established a bridgehead; the latter was attacked during the night by both German aircraft and a small ground assault supported by several tanks. It was also out of this bridgehead that the highly secretive, and controversial, Task Force Baum was launched en route to free American POWs at Oflag XIIIb at Hammelburg. This raid, which included C Company of the 37th Tank Battalion and A Company of the 10th Armored Infantry Battalion, was spotted and attacked in running gunfights by elements of the 36.Volksgrenadier-Division and replacement units belonging to the 251. Infanterie-Division. The Task Force operated 90km behind enemy lines and was sent in all probability to free Patton's son-in-law, Lieutenant-Colonel John Waters, who was held at the camp. While the raid was ultimately disastrous, it did deceive the Germans as to the exact direction that Patton's Third US Army was going to take during its next leap forward.

Even as the 4th Armored Division was racing to the Main River, to the west the 5th Infantry and 6th Armored divisions were pushing north toward Frankfurt. On March 25, Colonel John Hines' CCA of the 6th Armored passed Gross-Gerau, only to encounter a significant amount of direct fire from antiaircraft guns that forced his column off the major roads. By this stage of the war, the Germans were rapidly redeploying these guns for ground engagements, and many of those at the Frankfurt airport had already been removed and set up at important locations to provide fire support for roadblocks. Nevertheless, a number of guns remained in the vicinity of the airport, and CCA engaged in firefights with these as it pushed through woods and swamplands toward the Main River.

Hines halted to assess the situation near Mörfelden, and helped flush out some enemy infantry nearby. While talking on the radio, an 88mm round slammed into the back of his turret. Hines saw the flash and instinctively pulled on the hatch to close it, only to realize the fingers of his left hand had been blown off. As he sank into the turret, he also became aware that much of his lower face was shot up, yet calmly reported his injury to the division command post while scooping bone and shrapnel fragments from his throat with his right hand. Colonel Albert Harris, until then the CCR commander, took over by that evening for Hines, who was evacuated to the rear. Patton assessed that Hines' injury spooked the 6th Armored's leadership, and to snap them back to reality told Grow that if he did not get into Frankfurt that night that he would be relieved of command. As for Hines, he would survive the war despite a grim prognosis to be awarded the Distinguished Service Cross.

The next day, CCA doubled its efforts and pushed to the Main River just north of the airport. The first bridges they found had been destroyed, but Combat Team 15, led by Lieutenant-Colonel Embry Lagrew, found the main railroad bridge that led into the Frankfurt

Lieutenant-Colonel Creighton Abrams, the commander of CCB, 4th Armored Division. Abrams was known for his aggressive armor tactics. When he commanded the 37th Tank Battalion, it had one of the best kill-to-loss ratios of any in the European Theater of Operations. Abram's combat command would be called upon to send forth Task Force Baum in an effort to rescue Patton's son-in-law at a German camp. (US Army Signal Corps/The General George Patton Museum)

US 6TH ARMORED DIVISION'S COMBAT TEAM 9 ASSAULTS ACROSS THE SACHSENHAUSEN HIGHWAY BRIDGE INTO FRANKFURT, MARCH 26, 1945 (PP. 82–83)

Having breached the Rhine, US infantry and armor pushed to the Main River to capture important cities such as Frankfurt and Aschaffenburg. Led by the US 6th Armored Division, American troops found several bridges on March 25 only partially damaged, and began pushing troops across the Main to secure Frankfurt. Much of the attack was filmed by US Army combat cameramen.

As the 6th Armored Division, followed by the 5th Infantry Division advanced north on the Main River, they were engaged by antiaircraft guns, particularly 88s, positioned around the Frankfurt Flughafen (airport). Colonel John Hines, commander of the 6th Armored Division's CCA, was seriously wounded on 25 March, his position taken by Colonel Albert Harris.

The Germans considered the defense of Frankfurt crucial, and deciding that a change of command was necessary, they dispatched Oberstleutnant Erich Löffler, the defender of Koblenz, to take over the city defenses. As of March 25–26, Frankfurt was under the command of Generalmajor Friedrich Stemmermann, a reserve police officer. The garrison was composed of infantry replacement personnel, local Volksturm, and antiaircraft units. While some of the personnel had combat experience, they lacked cohesive training as a combat formation and some of the heavy equipment necessary for street fighting.

On 26 March, Combat Team 15, led by Lieutenant-Colonel Embry Lagrew, found a partially intact railroad bridge over the Main at Niederrad. As Lagrew prepared to cross the river, Combat Team 9, under the command of Major Gilman Morse, passed to the east and found a more suitable bridge at Sachsenhausen (**1**). The Americans decided to focus their efforts there, and by 1630hrs, the first troops from the 9th Armored Infantry Battalion were across the Main River.

The Sachsenhausen bridge was too damaged to support armor, but two M-5A1 Stuart tanks (**2**) positioned themselves on the bridge's approach to rake the opposite side with machine-gun fire. Under this fire support, and while under heavy German shelling, troops from the 5th Infantry Division's 11th Infantry Regiment (**3**) are shown joining the crossing. They will push into Frankfurt, advancing on the main railroad station near the Baseler Platz, harassed by sniper fire from desperate German defenders.

By March 27, the 5th Infantry Division had taken command of the bridgehead into Frankfurt, with the 6th Armored Division pulling back to assemble south of the river, prepared to engage in exploitation of any success.

On the morning of March 27, Löffler arrived to take command, even as his predecessor was wounded by an American artillery barrage. Löffler's tenure of command would last but three hours, as he would be mortally wounded by a similar barrage. The arrival of 11.Panzer Division in the area did little to prevent the city from falling, and by March 29, Frankfurt was cleared of German resistance.

Hauptbahnhof railroad station from Niederrad damaged but possibly usable. Lagrew immediately threw a company of infantry across the river. However, Combat Team 9, under Major Gilman Morse, advanced past Combat Team 15 on the right and found a highway bridge leading north out of Sachsenhausen that was not as damaged. The Americans shifted all of their energy to this site, and by 1630hrs most of the 9th Armored Infantry Battalion was across and into Frankfurt. Though too damaged to support heavy vehicles, a pair of M-5 Stuart tanks positioned themselves on the bridge's approach to rake the opposite side with machine-gun fire. Soon, troops from the 5th Infantry Division's 11th Regiment joined in, systematically probing northward to the Baseler Platz and the railroad station. Though almost a day late, Patton did not follow through with his threat to fire Grow.

The defense of Frankfurt was crucial to the German leadership, and despite the fact that he had not really provided staunch resistance in Koblenz, Löffler was named to be the new commander in Frankfurt. Currently under Generalmajor Friedrich Stemmermann, a reserve police officer, the Frankfurt garrison was composed of Infanterie-Ersatz-Bataillon 81, two other garrison battalions, an assortment of Volksturm, and supported by

American infantry advance toward Frankfurt along the Reichsautobahn, March 27. The lead soldier in the center is pointing at the cameraman, while the sign in the center of the photo points to an exit for "Frankfurt/Main South." The autobahn system had originally been built by the Nazi leadership to allow common Germans to travel the country, especially in the newly released Volkswagen that never truly reached the hands of consumers. Instead, the autobahn became the principle route of advance of invading Allied forces both west and east. Frankfurt would be completely cleared of major resistance by March 29. (NARA)

On March 27, 5th Infantry Division troops work to flush out snipers in Frankfurt. By this time, most serious resistance in the city had been vanquished, and a few hours later the recently appointed commander Oberstleutnant Erich Löffler would be mortally wounded by an American artillery barrage. Yet, pockets of resistance remained, and the heavily damaged condition of the city was prime real estate for German troops and Volksturm with sniper rifles and Panzerfausts. (NARA)

some antiaircraft batteries. On the morning of the 27th, Stemmermann was waiting by his car for Löffler to arrive when American artillery landed on his position and seriously wounded him. Löffler arrived shortly after, but his tenure in command would be very short. Three hours later, another salvo of American 105mm rounds slammed into his command post, leaving the new garrison commander mortally wounded and the defense of the city in confusion.

Even as Frankfurt was on the verge of falling, 11.Panzer-Division under Generalleutnant Wend von Wietersheim, was beginning to arrive in driblets in the area. Having been pulled out of the Remagen area on March 23, the division was alerted the next day to start moving south, a process that was easier said than done. By the time most of the division started out, Patton's 87th and 89th Infantry divisions had crossed the Rhine between Braubach and St Goarshausen, and were pushing east. In the process, they held up parts of Wietersheim's division as it tried to road-march south. The reconnaissance battalion arrived first, on the 26th, creating a security line between Frankfurt and Hanau. Panzergrenadier-Regiment 110 and the artillery arrived the next day after shaking off American forces pursuing them. In addition, elements of 6.SS-Gebirgs-Division "Nord," seemingly everywhere in this campaign, began to show up north of Frankfurt. All of this was assembled under Kniess' LXXXV.Armee-Korps. Once again, the measures came too late.

On March 28, the 317th Regiment of the 80th Infantry Division forced a crossing of the Rhine at Mainz and approached Frankfurt from the west. Wiesbaden was cleared that same day, and under pressure from two directions, Frankfurt fell on the 29th. With both the Rhine and Main rivers breached, and with major cities like Frankfurt, Aschaffenburg, and Hanau secured, Patton's Third US Army was poised to plunge into central Germany. It seemed incredible that just five weeks prior, the Third US Army was still pushing out of the Siegfried Line and crossing the Prüm River. Now, Patton's boys were driving hard into the heart of Germany itself, with the end of the war in Europe itself just five weeks away.

An M7 Priest self-propelled 105mm howitzer from the 22nd Field Artillery Battalion, 4th Armored Division continues the pursuit, crossing the Main River on March 28. Patton was concerned about crossing the Rhine at Nierstein–Oppenheim because his army would soon have to cross the Main. German commanders tried to make his fears a reality, hoping to slow Patton's army and blow the bridges over the river before they fell into American hands. Events proved Patton's fears to be unfounded. (NARA)

AFTERMATH

On the night of March 27, Generalmajor Oskar Munzel drove up to the burned-out shell of Ziegenberg Castle to report to Generalfeldmarschall Kesselring. Munzel, having just finished a tour on the Eastern Front and having been appointed as the commandant of the Panzer Training School at Bergen, had been tasked to take command of the Panzer "Thuringia" formation. This last-ditch scratch formation was built out of the Bergen school's staff and two training battalions, and was to also take in hand the remnants of 2.Panzer-Division whose commander, Lauchert, along with his entire staff, was listed as missing in action. Munzel was supposed to report to Hausser at Heeresgruppe G's headquarters, but as it was a circuitous trip, he decided to stop in on Kesselring first.

Munzel found Kesselring alone save for his chief of staff, General Siegfried Westphal. The rest of the staff had already been evacuated to the east, heading to their new headquarters site, and Kesselring and Westphal were about to leave as well. The Generalfeldmarschall had chosen to stay at Ziegenberg, even after the air attack on March 19, in an effort to bolster the morale of his men. Even as Munzel arrived, intermittent fighting was ongoing to the west as elements of 6.SS-Gebirgs-Division "Nord" engaged in a fierce fighting withdrawal against Patton's VIII Corps after they had crossed the Rhine at Boppard and Oberwesel. Kesselring promptly suspended the need for Munzel to report to Hausser, assigning him at once to support Obstfelder's hard-pressed 7.Armee. He also provided him with a basic overview of the tactical situation.

At this point, the First US Army had broken out of the Remagen bridgehead and was rapidly advancing to the east. Montgomery's 21st Army Group had already crossed the Rhine in strength to the north of the Ruhr,

Troops climbing aboard a DUKW at the Oberwesel crossing site, March 26. DUKWs, pronounced "ducks" by the soldiers, were used extensively for both river and ocean shore amphibious operations, despite their instability while afloat and tendency to overturn. It is interesting to note that in most of the photos of Patton's Rhine crossing, a medic appears prominent in them. Moreover, most of the men also seem to be lacking life preservers, even though they were available in quantity. (NARA)

Into the heart of Germany, March 22–April 4, 1945

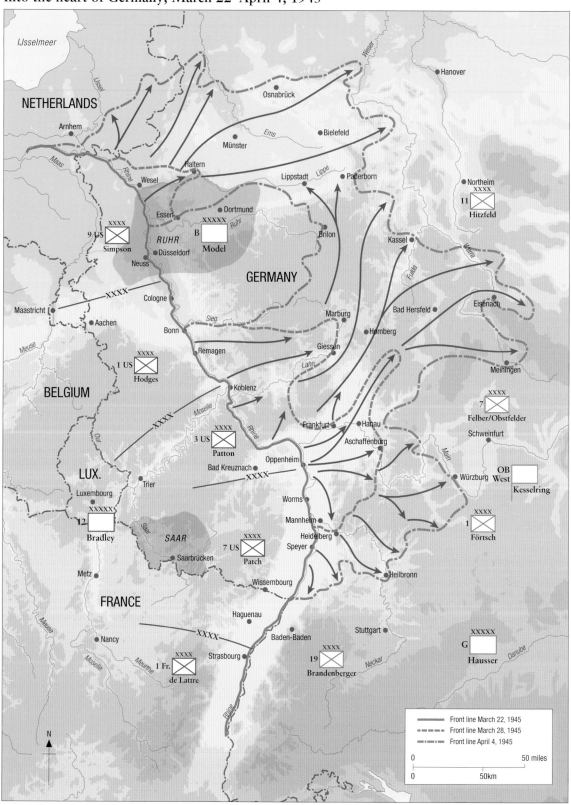

and together with the First US Army, was on the verge of surrounding the Ruhr, which would deprive Germany of its remaining industrial base. To the south and west, Patton's Third Army was rolling both east and north; the latter thrust would soon create a pocket east of the Rhine in the Vogelsberg region north of Frankfurt. And to round out the list of disasters, Devers' 6th US Army Group was on the verge of crossing the Rhine as well, which would allow American and French divisions to plunge into southern Germany. With the Rhine River line irrevocably lost, the leading German generals all knew that the war could only end in utter defeat.

What was Munzel to do? Over the next few days, he would assemble the most motley organization imaginable: school cadre and students; infantry training formations without heavy weapons; panzer training units with no tanks—the only one they had breaking down en route; even a Flak brigade without guns, which had been ambushed by an American armored column while rail loaded. Overall, Munzel was able to assemble about 4,000 men, most of them young recruits with minimal training, and seven Jagdpanzer 38 Hetzers and three tanks. He had no artillery, no supply organization, and even the field kitchens were few and far between. His men had but the bare essentials of small arms and a few panzerfausts. The handful of trucks he had were wood-burning vehicles, and he had no communications to speak of. To control this mélange of humanity, Munzel would have to dash between them in his command car. The persistent lack of fuel meant that he would more likely have to coordinate their movements on foot. There would not even be time to train them into any semblance of a fighting force, for Obstfelder would demand their immediate commitment to combat.

After infantry from the 6th Armored Division secured a crossing of the Main River at Sachsenhausen, allowing the Americans to push into Frankfurt, troops of the 5th Infantry Division probed the streets of the Baseler Platz, just a few blocks from the main railroad station, for German snipers. Today in the Baseler Platz, the nightmare of combat has been replaced by the confusion of racing traffic and pedestrians passing various shops and restaurants. While the building to the right was later torn down and replaced by a modern-looking office complex, the one at center remains to this day. (NARA)

Even as Patton's army was exploiting its crossing at Nierstein–Oppenheim, other units of his command, like the 87th Infantry Division seen here at Boppard on March 27, made additional crossings. Boppard had been previously used by the Germans to evacuate elements of Höhne's LXXXIX.Armee-Korps, including the 6.SS-Gebirgs-Division "Nord" that later reappeared north of Frankfurt. The Third US Army also made crossings at Oberwesel and St Goarshausen. (NARA)

Thus rode into combat the shadow of 2.Panzer-Division, a once-famous formation now reduced to fighting on foot in the center of a dying nation, a symbol of what was now the German Wehrmacht. Munzel would later put his bravest face on it, but the reality was bleak to the point of utter despair, waiting for the end to come. He would remain in command until being wounded on April 3, relinquishing control to Oberst Karl Stollbrock, who would command the "division" until the end of the war, first as part of Osterkamp's provisional XII.Armee-Korps until April 25, and then under LXXXV.Armee-Korps of General Smilo Freiherr von Lüttwitz for one last gasp in the Thuringian Mountains.

Even before Munzel met with Kesselring, the morning of the 27th found Private First Class Malcom Fletcher and his companions of the 101st Regiment of Paul's 26th Infantry Division paddling their way across the Main River near Hanau. They crossed under machine-gun fire, which Fletcher recalled was "an experience I do not want to repeat." On the opposite bank, they clawed their way out of the mud and quickly cleaned out German positions set up to delay their advance. Fletcher grimly noted: "there is only one thing to do—wipe them out," though he still felt sorry for them (Fletcher 2011, p. 117). They pushed on to the east, still taking casualties. The weather was warm and sunny—a beautiful morning.

Late in the afternoon of that 27th of March, Lieutenant-Colonel Irzyk and his 8th Tank Battalion of the 4th Armored Division was ready to

Endgame: Tanks of the 11th Armored Division ford a stream deep inside Germany as the pursuit continues until the Nazi Reich is at last finished. One German soldier, when writing home to his wife, noted that the war would only come to an end when the last German unit in the last corner of the Reich was broken. (US Army Signal Corps/The General George Patton Museum)

cross the Main River at Klein-Auheim and move into Hanau. By 1900hrs, the entire battalion was over the river, and with accompanying infantry began to clear the roadblocks out of the city. Irzyk took stock of the fact that Hanau was 17km east of Frankfurt: "So the Americans had unquestionably reached the heartland of Germany" (Irzyk 1996, p. 352). By the next day, the 4th Armored Division was pushing through the security line of 11.Panzer-Division on its way northeast toward Kassel, with its commander Wietersheim barely avoiding capture outside of Hanau.

With Mainz and Frankfurt secure, Third US Army engineers rebuilt the destroyed railroad bridge across the Rhine at Mainz. Patton dedicated the bridge by cutting the ribbon with a bayonet on April 14, with the bridge named after President Franklin Roosevelt, who had just passed away two days prior. Present to Patton's left is Major-General Ewart Plank of Communications Zone (COMZ) and behind him is Colonel Harry Hulen, who supervised its construction. Hulen had the bridge built in 9 days, 18 hours, and 10 minutes, yet was apologetic because Julius Caesar built his Rhine River bridge in 12 hours less. Patton made a point to Hulen that Caesar had not built a railroad bridge. (US Army Signal Corps/The General George Patton Museum)

Major Grillenberger, the intrepid commander of the Jagdtigers of schwere Panzerjäger-Abteilung 653 was accused of "tactical blunders" in the face of the enemy. Despite all his previous efforts, he was busted in rank to Leutnant and relieved of command on March 25, being replaced by Major Rolf Fromme. Grillenberger was transferred to schwere Panzer-Abteilung 507 with Tiger IIs, where he served as a platoon leader east of the Ruhr Pocket until the unit was so starved of equipment that they had to settle for Jadgpanzer 38 Hetzers and a few PzKpfw IVs before surrendering.

And what of Lauchert? Disgusted and disillusioned by the incompetence he saw in the conduct of the war, he separated from the others who swam the Rhine and walked east to his home in Bamberg, dodging roving military police patrols and traveling by foot over 250km, where he waited out the end of the war with his wife. After the war, he survived accusations of being a war criminal, and later landed a role as a key military advisor for the 1965 Hollywood movie, *Battle of the Bulge*. During production, he provided actor Robert Shaw with his own medals to wear. Many years after the filming, Lauchert was cited by actor James MacArthur as the quintessential gentleman, "simply the classic soldier."

That night, with his meeting at Ziegenberg complete, Munzel climbed into his staff car and headed out into the dark in search of Osterkamp's headquarters. One thing was certainly clear. German decision-making had always been too little and too late, though considering the circumstances, much would have not ultimately changed in the end. Nevertheless, Patton, his field commanders, and especially the staff officers were always one step ahead of the Germans in the decision-making process, and this made a big difference as to who won or lost, but more importantly, who lived or died. With Munzel on the road, Kesselring and Westphal soon followed shortly after—the last of the last from a bombed-out castle, heading off to the east to their new headquarters deep within a railroad tunnel near Schloss Reinhardsbrunn, east of Fulda, with Private First Class Fletcher, Lieutenant-Colonel Irzyk, Weyland's pilots, General Patton, and the entire American army inexorably nipping at their heels.

THE BATTLEFIELD TODAY

Walking along the Baseler Strasse towards the main railroad station in Frankfurt, one can still see patched-up pockmarks along the walls of buildings caused by small-arms fire during the advance of the 6th Armored Division's infantry into the city. Today, the street is a bustling thoroughfare, lined with shops and restaurants passed by people who seem oblivious to what happened there just 75 years ago. The Moselle River is now a tourist's delight, with steeply inclined vineyards and charming castles visited mostly by people from Great Britain and the Netherlands. It is difficult to picture that a desperate action took place between 90th Infantry riflemen and 6.SS-Gebirgs-Division "Nord" mountain troopers in Alken, beneath the lovely twin towers of Thurant Castle.

The woods north of Gross-Gerau are today plied by thousands of locals who walk and cycle its roads and trails, again apparently oblivious to the events of 75 years ago. The small forest house where General Runge set up his headquarters has been since torn down, replaced by the Helen-Keller-Schule. One can only wonder how many of the children playing on the soccer field know of what happened there. Ziegenberg Castle, a total ruin by war's end, was gradually rebuilt save for the outlying structures and bunkers, which were razed. It is today a privately owned residence, while nearby and tucked in the woods just up the road lies the remains of Hitler's Adlerhorst, blocked off by fences.

Dexheim, west of Nierstein, is nestled in a valley whose surrounding hills were once the assembly area for tens of thousands of American tanks, half-tracks, and trucks. Today it is a peaceful village with narrow streets and more trendy houses bedecked with solar panels on the outer edges. Nierstein and Oppenheim are enjoyable towns to visit, in particular due to the wine production there. Above Oppenheim, the ruins of Landskrone Castle provide a spectacular view of Patton's crossing site to the east. Along the riverfront there is hardly any indication that at one time the town was overflowing with American soldiers, though there are photographs of the event in the offices of the Louis Guntrum Winery in Nierstein, where Patton had set up a temporary office once the bridgehead was secure.

However, if one looks a little closer, one can find evidence of the war. On the west bank in Nierstein is a commemorative marker placed in 2017 by the 249th Engineer Combat Battalion Association and the town of Nierstein to honor one of the bridging units that assisted in the crossing. And on the other side of the river, tucked away up a back road to the north of the main route heading east from the ferry site, is a stone memorial set up in 1954, listing the names of five men and one woman arrested for their refusal to perform military construction work to counter the American advance. These individuals were shot for their resistance, which serves as both a terrible indictment of the cruelty of some, and a sobering reminder of the courage of others caught in the middle between an irresistible force and an immovable object. Dedicated in 1954, today it remains largely unknown, though a handful of locals continue to place wreaths and flowers astride the marker. Only a small street sign directs you to the site.

A little known monument to a brave few who refused to be press-ganged into building earthworks to defend the Rhine from attack. After listing their names, five men and the wife of one of the men, the inscription reads: "21 March 1945. In view of their homes, the innocent were shot. In memory of their death! To the living a reminder! What happened here must never be repeated." While set up in 1954, it is largely unknown today, with a small road sign pointing the way. Yet, true to form for many monuments in Germany, a small group of locals continues to adorn it with wreathes and flowers. (Author's collection)

FURTHER READING

Most of the published material available on the Third US Army's crossing of the Rhine at Nierstein–Oppenheim is from American sources. Unpublished unit histories and after-action reports, along with studies conducted by German officers after the war, offer a reasonably descriptive picture of the event. However, photographs from the German side are few and far between, which is understandable as most armies rarely photograph themselves during periods of defeat. The following sources would be useful not only to those studying the operation in greater depth, but also to wargamers who wish to simulate the campaign, especially when developing the orders of battle. In particular, a good working knowledge of the German Ersatzheer (Replacement Army) is essential to understanding the organization of the German combat groups assembled in the last months of the war. Naturally, inclusion of any sources, including websites, does not constitute any endorsement of particular ideological beliefs.

Published accounts and secondary sources

Afiero, Massimiliano (trans. Ralph Riccio), *The 6th Waffen-SS Gebirgs (Mountain) Division Nord*, Atglen, PA: Schiffer Publishing Ltd, 2017

Bradley, Omar N., *A Soldier's Story*, New York: The Modern Library, 1999

Codman, Charles, *Drive*, Boston: Little, Brown and Co., 1957

D'Este, Carlo, *Patton: A Genius for War*, New York: Harper Collins, 1995

Fletcher, Malcolm, *Not for Morbidity's Sake: A World War II Yankee Division War Diary*, np, 2011

Glantz, David and Heiber, Helmut (eds.), *Hitler and His Generals: Military Conferences 1942–1945*, New York: Enigma Books, 2004

Groh, Richard, *The Dynamite Gang: The 367th Fighter Group in World War II*, Fallbrook, CA: Aero Publishers, Inc., 1983

Irzyk, Albin, *He Rode Up Front for Patton*, Raleigh, NC: Pentland Press, Inc., 1996

Kursietis, Andris J., *The Wehrmacht at War, 1939–1945: The Units and Commanders of the German Ground Forces during World War II*, Soesterberg, Netherlands: Aspekt, 1999

MacDonald, Charles B., *The Last Offensive: The United States Army in World War II: The European Theater of Operations*, Washington, DC: Office of the Chief of Military History, 1973

Patton, George S. Jr. (ed. Martin Blumenson), *The Patton Papers*, Vol. II, Boston: Houghton Mifflin Co., 1974

——, *War as I Knew It*, New York: The Great Commanders, 1994

Pettibone, Charles D., *The Organization and Order of Battle of Militaries in World War II*, Vol. I: *Germany*, Victoria, Canada: Trafford Publishing, 2006

Price, Alfred, *The Luftwaffe Data Book*, London: Greenhill Books, 1997

Spires, David N., *Air Power for Patton's Army: The XIX Tactical Air Command in the Second World War*, Washington, DC: Air Force History Museum Program, 2002

Weigley, Russell F., *Eisenhower's Lieutenants: The Campaign of France and Germany, 1944–1945*, Bloomington: Indiana University Press, 1981

Unpublished studies and reports
US Army
Third US Army After-Action Report
XIX Tactical Air Command, *Tactical Air Operations in Europe: A Report on the Employment of the XIX TAC, 1 Aug 1944–9 May 1945*
5th Infantry Division and Regimental/Battalion After-Action Reports
4th Armored Division and Battalion After-Action Reports
90th Infantry Division After-Action Reports
Seventh US Army After-Action Report
Dyer, Lieutenant-Colonel George, *XII Corps, Spearhead of Patton's Third Army*, New Hope, PA: XII Corps History Association, 1947
Liddel, Major Robert, et al, *Rhine River Crossing Conducted by the Third US Army and the Fifth Infantry Division, 22–24 March 1945*, CSI Battlebook 19-A. Fort Leavenworth, KS: Combat Studies Institute, 1984
Military Headquarters and Installations in Germany, Washington DC: Military Intelligence Division, War Department, February 1945
Office of the Engineer, *Crossing the Rhine River by Third US Army* (nd)
Order of Battle of the German Army, Washington DC: Military Intelligence Division, War Department, March 1945
The German Replacement Army (Ersatzheer), Washington, DC: Military Intelligence Division, War Department, April 1944

Postwar studies by German officers
The below manuscripts (with the exception of the entry for Schmid, Joseph) are from the European Theater Historical Interrogations (ETHINT) of senior German personalities in the immediate postwar period. The manuscript number is given in parenthesis at the end of each ETHINT entry.
Alberti, Konrad von, *Kampfgruppe Albert (1–28 Apr 45) and Battle Sector XII (Wehrkreis XII) South (15–25 Mar 45)* (B-585)
Baltzer, Martin, *Bewegungen der Division Nr. 172 März/April 1945* (B-126)
Beyer, Franz, *The Final Fighting of the LXXX Army Corps from the Marne to the Danube* (B-082)
——, *LXXX Corps, Aug 1944–Apr 1945* (B-320)
Bölsen, Hans, *Battle Sector XII (Wehrkreis XII), 7–21 Mar 1945* (B-063)
——, *Kampfgruppe Runge, 22–26 Mar 1945* (B-406)
Brenner, Karl, *6th SS Mountain Division, 1–19 March 1945* (B-693)
——, *6th SS Gebirgs Division Nord During Defensive Combat, 19 March–3 April 1945* (B-715)
Bürcky, Heinrich, *The 159 Infantry Division in the Rhineland Campaign, 1 Dec–21 Mar 1945* (B-150)
——, *The 159 Infantry Division in the Campaign of Central Germany, 22 Mar–4 Apr 1945* (B356)
Fäckenstedt, Earnst F., *The Campaign in Central Germany from 22 Mar–11 May 45* (B-404)
——, *The Activities of the Western Wehrkreis from September 1944 to March 1945* (B-665)
Felber, Hans, *The Seventh Army, 20 Feb–26 Mar 1945* (B-831)
Gersdorf, Rudolf Freiherr von, *Between the Westwall and the Rhine, 7th Army During the Period 1 Feb–21 Mar 1945* (B-123)
——, *Final Phase of the War: From the Rhine to the Czech Border* (B-893)
Hausser, Paul, *Army Group G, 25 Jan–21 Mar 1945* (B-600)
Höhne, Gustav, *Fighting of the LXXXIX Army Corps, 10–16 March 1945* (B-377)
——, *LXXXIX Corps, 18–28 Mar 1945* (B-584)
Krüger, H.H., *Rhein–Main 23–28 March 1945* (B-324)
Munzel, Oskar, *2d Panzer Division, 28 Mar–4 Apr 1945* (B-360)
Oriola, Ralph Graf von, *The Rhineland Campaign, 18 Feb–21 Mar 1945* (B-052)
——, *XIII Corps Campaign Central Germany, 22–31 Mar 1945* (B-392)
Osterkamp, Herbert, *Feldzug Rheinland 16 Sept 1944–21 März 1945* (B-119)
——, *Feldzug Mittel-Deustchland 22–31 März 1945* (B-405)
Schmid, Joseph "Beppo," *Luftwaffe Operations in the West, 1943–1945, Vol. IV, Sept. 44–May 45 (Air Force Historical Series)* (AFD-090519-015)
Schramm, Percy, *OKW War Diary* (C-20)
Wietersheim, Wend von, *11th Tank Division between the Rhine and the Czech Border, Part I: 21 Mar–15 Apr 1945* (B-755)
Wilutzki, Horst, *Army Group G, 22 Mar–6 May 1945* (B-703)

INDEX

Figures in **bold** refer to illustrations.